TOOLS
FOR
SURVIVAL

A GUIDE FOR BUSINESS OPPORTUNITIES
AND CAREER SKILLS

MARTHA HARRIS FAIR
HARRIS ACADEMY
2402 South Newberry Court
Denver, Colorado   80222
2nd Edition

Library of Congress Catalog Card No. 82-084130

ISBN: 0-911181-00-8 paperback

ACKNOWLEDGMENTS

This book is dedicated to those who gave me what I needed to assure my survival:

> My father, Hiawatha Roosevelt Harris,
> My mother, Ethel Ragsdale Harris,
> My daughter, Jamila Harris, and
> My son, Hiawatha Abdul Hagg.

I give special thanks to Charlie Winton who welcomed the second edition and helped me to understand the shelf appeal of a cover and to Vicki Webb who designed the new cover. Jamila edited the manuscript and wouldn't let me stop. Another writer Douglas Anderson and his loving wife Mabel rolled up their sleeves.

TABLE OF CONTENTS

Preface

I started this book many times by writing articles, by making public appearances and speeches, and by counseling many students, displaced homemakers, minorities, and women in the world of work. Every time I made such an effort, and then tried to work on the book, I found that I needed another piece of information, another dialogue with a person in the work force, or most importantly, I found that I needed another personal experience. The added experiences that I needed were characterized by my need to do more reality testing. My test question was usually "Is that all there is?," or "How can I be sure that this will work for others?"

By age thirty, my resume had to be squeezed onto one page because I had been blessed by involvement in a variety of job opportunities. I had worked consistently and had earned outstanding performance evaluations. Yet, my resume read like an Agatha Christie novel, without the whodunit portion, but with all of the what-for questions. My resume is proof that I had done all of the outdated, overrated "ought-to's." I had responded to the "ought to go to college" though only sixteen years old, the "ought to get married" sure or not, the "ought to have children" though I didn't want them, the "ought to accept a teaching position" even though I was a trained scientist, and the "ought to get a Master's Degree" because that would entitle me to a salary increase. None of the "ought-to's" were based on any up-to-date personal assessment or any rank order of choices from a wide variety of opportunities. The males that I worked with went from being fourth grade teachers to becoming principals, superintendents, athletic directors, and city comptrollers. I felt trapped in the traditional goals and in the stereotypical roles as I had fallen prey to the safety of the "ought-to's."

The consequence of using the aimless "ought-to's" for making career choices and for guiding skills building was that at age thirty I found myself unhappy, underpaid, overworked, and not appreciated. I had no clues as to how I arrived in that position. I had not planned nor applied any strategies for my arrival. Many intelligent and capable Black people whom I know also found themselves showing up for work every day for many years and then one day crying hysterically, drinking extensively, taking pills regularly, and/or exhibiting fits of rage about ordinary occurrences. We now know these symptoms to be indicators of the phenomenon *career burnout*. By whatever name, I began to wonder about correlative factors that contributed to such a destructive result for so many Black workers.

This book is about the cause-effect relationships and the discoveries that I made about the survival of minority and women workers in the American labor force based on twenty-five years of hard work. The reader will find the phrase minorities and women workers throughout the text. The term minorities is defined as both males and females of varied ethnic backgrounds. Women means persons of the female gender, with the emphasis being on Caucasian females. Where the term minority workers is used, that reference connotes workers whose numbers are the smallest in particular agencies, institutions, and organizations.

My daughter, who is a college graduate with two years' additional graduate study, spent six years in administrative positions in governmental agencies before she also became a victim of career burnout. As we talked and reviewed organizational structure, decision-making models, the power-politics of relationships, and needs systems of individuals, we found no generation gap in the survival strategies that had worked for her. One of our strategies was a tactic called *guerrilla warfare*. We found guerrilla warfare a viable tool for women and minorities who sought to control their career paths and to apply new techniques to CYA, Cover Your A___ (Anatomy). We discovered in our experiences many other valuable *Tools for Survival*.

This book will help minorities and women to make some new career choices, to recognize and deal with stress, to obtain a job, to keep it until it has served its purpose, and move on to a better work experience using these *Tools for Survival*. Although this book addresses some of the unique challenges faced by Black workers, it is the author's hope that the book will serve as a resource for American workers throughout the world of work.

Martha Harris Fair

Tools for Survival

Introduction

The positive approach is the only successful approach to survival for minorities and women in the work force. Contrary to beliefs that positive thinking is a religion or religious doctrine, positive thinking and visualization are key tools for survival.

In order to absorb and to use a practical strategy for dealing with the numerous and specific challenges that minorities and women face in the work force, we must be determined to become experts in positive thinking. We must see ourselves as victorious and no longer victims in the work force. We must resolve that positive thoughts elicit positive results for survival as workers or employees in the American work force.

The book uses examples of Black Americans in work situations; although the author also provides emphases on survival for minorities and women. The author has observed and experienced some challenges that are indigenous to the Black female's efforts to survive in a labor force which is dominated by males. Strategies for survival must be amended and/or qualified for the Black female due to the man-made prescriptions for the traditional "usefulness" of females in the labor force. The Black female must identify, understand, and acknowledge the challenge to her femaleness and her race in the world of work in order to survive.

The book is written based on the assumption that it would serve as a how-to guide for both entry-level and experienced minorities and women workers. It is also the hope of the author that this book will inspire formal and informal interactions, conversations, and sharing of critical incidences among minorities and women. No matter what our levels or our endeavors, in America, minorities and women experience more similar experiences than they do different ones.

The redefinition of several traditional terms used by employers in the work force is necessary for development of a realistic survival plan for minorities and women. Workers must formulate understandings of the relevance of terms such as success, management, and job security. The assumptions underlying these terms are realistically re-evaluated in this book and tailored for a vision that will assist minorities and women in efforts to make gains rather than lose ground in the world of work.

The criteria used for determining career choice decisions made by prospective and experienced minority and women workers are re-examined in this book. Suggested career choice patterns are based on factual evidence and real-life experiences of real workers. For instance, Black Americans who decide to pursue law careers should be aware that their strategies for obtaining the law degree must prepare them for the challenges. Some of the challenges to be considered are the demands of gaining admission into professional school; completion of courses taught by racist and sexist professors; passing the state bar exam, in which Blacks experience an 85% first time failure rate based on race; the obstacles of establishing private practice, or the less likely opportunity with a large firm; and the median salaries received by Blacks and women in law rather than the illustrious salaries earned by a small percentage of the dominant group—caucasian males. Notice the word is challenges, *not* insurmountable obstacles. Utilizing the positive action plan strategy outlined in this book, women and minority individuals who decide to become lawyers CAN DO IT and SURVIVE!

This book is an instrument to be used by minorities and women who wish to develop successful patterns of employment. Survival in the work force is success for minorities and women who work to provide fulfillment of their human needs as individuals, as families, and as communities.

Roslyn Jamila Harris
Editor

You Can Do It!

CHAPTER ONE

CHAPTER ONE

"I find the great thing in this world is not so much where we stand as in what direction we are moving."
— *Oliver Wendell Holmes*

Positive Thinking for Survival

The positive action plan of survival for minorities and women in the work force is three-dimensional. Our innermost thoughts are housed in the first dimension, our subconscious; our attitudes, in the second; and our actions, which determine approaches to the challenge of living, formulate the third dimension.

The power of your *subconscious* is key, and *not* your intellectual, rational, conscious mind as the socialization process tells us. "What is impressed in the subconscious is expressed in your actions."[1] Your subconscious mind controls all your physical involuntary functions such as heartbeat and blood circulation. Your subconscious works continuously and unceasingly, whereas the conscious mind rests during states of relaxation and sleep.

The subconscious mind that is impressed with good thoughts produces good attitudes and actions. When we impress our subconscious with positive thoughts, the manifestation in our lives is positive attitudes, positive actions, and positive results.

#1   **TOOL FOR SURVIVAL**

Use the power of positive thought action so that your mind can practice success.

Believe in yourself. Believe in all of your positive thoughts, positive attitudes, and positive approaches to facing challenges. Have faith in the power of the spoken word. Talk back confidently to fear and doubt. Expect the best and get it. You can do it!

Practice Patterns of Success

There are specific techniques that we use to impress our subconscious minds with thoughts for survival and success. "Believe in Yourself!"[2] Self-confidence in your decision-making, and confidence that you make the best of *all* experiences in the work force and in your life, are very important.

When we make decisions confidently about our desires in the world of work and our lives, we discipline our imaginations to visualize the results we want. A disciplined imagination is a vehicle for impressing images on the subconscious mind. When we decide that we want to have a positive attitude, we visualize ourselves smiling, happy, walking with lighthearted rhythm, and expressing a positive attitude. We feed our subconscious continually with positive thoughts of self-confidence and triumph. If you need to purchase some books, write the order or the check for the books. Do not allow your thoughts to imagine a lack of adequate funds. Picture yourself reading the books, and using the material from them.

We often say that a picture is worth a thousand words. We are presented with examples of the power of language, and the printed word as we watch nations evolve and revolutions erupt. What about the *personal* power of the spoken word? Florence Scovel Shinn writes:

> God is man's supply and people can release, through their spoken word, all that belongs to them by divine right. You must have perfect faith in your spoken word.[3]

If we ask for success and prepare for failure, we get the situation for which we have prepared. In the Bible, the prophet Elisha told the three kings in the desert who asked for water to make this valley full of ditches. Even though they saw no rain or wind, the men were told to prepare for the thing for which they asked when there was not the slightest sign of it. Having made a statement of high spiritual truth, one challenges old beliefs in the subconscious and using denials "error is exposed to be put out."[4]

Through the daily use of affirmations we exercise our faith in the spoken word. An affirmation is a statement of future action put into the present tense, so that our subconscious can make future goals into present realities. Affirmation is a valuable technique for achieving success. Your most positive thoughts are reaffirmed daily.

If you need a new dwelling, you must speak words about moving into the right apartment or the right home. If you need a new job, begin to speak words about going to the right employer at the right time and the right salary. Your words guide you to being open and ready to receive the answer to your prayers.

#2 **TOOLS FOR SURVIVAL**

Use daily affirmations so that your subconscious can set into motion the desires of your heart.

Have faith in the power of the spoken word.

Know that all positive words establish the positive flow of events.

Remind yourself aloud that you are born to succeed, not to fail.

Prayer is the catalyst for spiritual treatment. Luke 18:1 says, "men ought always to pray and not to faint." The Science of Mind textbook explains spiritual treatment to mean that "Treatment is not willing things to happen; it is to provide within ourselves an avenue through which they may happen."[5]

A spiritual treatment is not a prayer of petition in which we ask the Great Spirit to do something for us. Rather, in treatment we reason from the premise that God is all there is, and we are a part of that Allness. We know that what we desire already exists within the Divine Nature. For the desire to be expressed in our personal lives, we need only to prepare a way for it to move into our personal thoughts and into our lives. In accord with these beliefs, we affirm that it has already happened in our experience. We should previsualize the events happening and recognize our joyous reaction to the experience as if it is already happening. The next step is to release the mental picture and to go about our affairs confidently, believing that our desire is coming at the right time.

#3   TOOLS FOR SURVIVAL

Use spiritual treatment to show that the Universe responds to us when we comply with the Law of Life.

STEPS FOR TREATMENT:

1. Decide exactly what you want.
2. Pray for your heart's desire.
3. Handle one idea at a time.
4. Do not try to change from pauper to prince overnight.
5. Know that your heart's desire is already on the way.
6. Visualize your joyful feelings, while receiving your desire.
7. Release your mental picture and go about your affairs confidently.

The level of expectation that we bring to a situation determines to a great extent the outcome in the situation. Always expect the best! A young man who had a past history of failure had suddenly experienced success in his life. When questioned about the cause of this positive change in his life, he responded: "Really it is quite simple. I merely learned the magic of believing. I discovered that if you expect the worst you will get the worst, and if you expect the best you will get the best. . ."[6]

The positive approach to survival in the work force for minorities and women is a dynamic process that is never ending. There are always new challenges, new heights, and new avenues of achievement in survival that allow us to use our positive approach as a way of life.

#4 TOOLS FOR SURVIVAL

Take a chance!

Minorities and women must take a chance in order to get a chance.

Remember that when fear closes a door, faith will open another door. If you open enough doors, one will be the right door. Go ahead, take a chance.

Remember that in nature the creatures with no backbone have the hardest shells. Go ahead, take a chance to get a chance to make a living and to care for yourself.

When an experience on our present job has served its purpose in our development, we move on to the next experience with positive enthusiasm for the lessons that are before us. Remember when you frowned at your grandmother who said, "Everything happens for the best?" At that time, it seemed like the ravings of a crazy old woman. Now you look back and hear what she meant with more understanding. What about the old folks you hear say, "Just keep on living, child. You'll understand why I am telling you this one day." Many times you hear those voices again and appreciate the loving guidance they tried to give, but you were too inexperienced to value.

We are born with what it takes to become "Overcomers". During our struggles, we must understand the power of our thoughts, attitudes, and actions. When we learn to use and control them and stop permitting our minds to dwell on the negative side of things, we will have taken the steps toward becoming successful Overcomers!

Overcomers are people who have learned some things about successes. Small successes become building blocks and stepping stones to new events that lead to more success. The notion that there is a "sweet smell" to success becomes a part of the behavior and needs system of the overcomer. Once people have known the feeling of elation, have had the rush of acceptance, or have experienced the sweet smell of success, they will seek to repeat patterns and behaviors that result in those peak responses. In other words, overcomers practice success.

> Recite affirmations daily to permit your mind to dwell on the positive side of things.
>
> Speak the words of an Overcomer.
> For example, try this affirmation the next time you've misplaced something . . . Nothing is ever lost. That thing or something better is on the way to me.

You can make up your personally tailored affirmations or you can share those used by others. Some affirmations that have helped me to center myself, to find peace, and to keep moving are listed here.

- Thank God for the unlimited increase in my mind and affairs.
- I let go and let God.
- I am poised and centered in Divine Mind, and nothing can disturb the calm peace of my soul.
- The spirit of the Lord goes before me, making safe, smooth, successful and helpful my way.

My favorite affirmation is **God is in charge!**

Leo Hauser, who speaks for the Personal Dynamics Institute, has recommended five steps for success. These steps compare favorably with the four list method for "Making Your Dreams Come True by the Unity Minister Sallye Taylor. The combined list and recommendations are as follows:

1. Know what your dream would look like if it would come true. Want your dream! Visualize your success.
2. List those things that you are good at and those things that you are not so good at doing. Take this inventory before there is a catastrophe. You must know what you do well.
3. Take the things that you are good at and find activities which provide opportunities for you to do those things. Exercise and practice your strengths even if it is an avocation at first start. Have some fun!
4. Write your goal down on paper. Then shoot for the moon! Set

big goals for yourself, then go after your goal an inch at a time.

By the yard it is hard.

By the inch it's a cinch.

Put each inch together, one at a time, adding them up until you have reached your goal.

#6   **TOOLS FOR SURVIVAL**

It takes a lot of slow to grow!

Positive Thinking and Race

The authorities on the power of positive thinking such as Norman Vincent Peale and Bob Conklin seldom deal with race as a factor. However, they both assert that the power of positive thinking has been used to overcome obstacles of great magnitude. Both authors agree that life is a composite of thoughts and ideas. Only when those thoughts allow negative lack ideas to work do negative manifestations appear.

Was it Abraham Lincoln and the signing of the Emancipation Proclamation that freed Blacks in America? Or did freedom emerge as the assertiveness of Black folks who affirmed that "I'm goin' to study war no more," and "Sing-a-song, full of faith that the dark past has taught us," and "We shall overcome." Historians agree that many intangible factors led to the 13th Amendment of the Constitution of the United States of America. Because the history of Africa and the history of the settlement of America are not written together, some of the factors slip away.

Upon examination, we find that Black Americans brought with them an old and rich heritage including royal families, complex governmental and finance systems, and an intense set of spiritual beliefs. The spiritual beliefs were based on combinations of the teachings of Islam and the Koran, the customs in ancestor worship, and the prophecies in the Bible. The spiritual factors are maintained within our culture and were used to oversee the general welfare of the people. Dr. Chancellor Williams has stated that we are forming strong organizations whose purposes are to become producers for the whole race. Further, Dr. Williams wrote:

We can do it. We've got to have the vision of our forefathers who built the pyramids.[7]

When Black Americans remember that we are the descendants of the dynasty of Pharoahs who built the great pyramids, we know that race provides a foundation for positive thinking. How can Blacks continue to thrive in America? Black Americans survived slavery. Though there were slave codes giving permission to beat, cut, maim, disfigure, and separate Black families, we survived. We have survived the Jim Crow laws that were established for the sole purpose of denying Black citizens rights to education, employment, and housing. Our nation has decided to reverse its position on integration for equality. Yet, Blacks survived the "separate but equal" period, and will survive the present retrenchment. Blacks continue to thrive and to excel though rape, murder, and lynching were crimes that were more often done against them than Caucasians. We have held positive thoughts before and after Reconstruction about our needs to be represented and to participate in politics.

Black Americans had positive thoughts about their actions when they were awarded 40 acres and a mule. Positive thoughts brought about migration to the north for the purpose of participating in the urbanization of industrial America. Blacks continued to think positively no matter how locked into urban poverty they found themselves. Though the facts seemed negative, Black people looked for truth and found positive results. Even when the appearance in fact was that a southern President probably would not be a Civil Rights advocate, the truth was that Lyndon Baines Johnson became an advocate for powerful, earthshaking civil rights legislation. The positive thinkers, civil rights leaders, used their cultural beliefs that said among other things, "things will get better," and "the darkest hour is just before the dawn."

Getting into the spiritual swing of things is no easy matter for Blacks or for Caucasians. Yet, there are differences in how we use the cultural understandings and the spiritual symbols to promote positive thinking, attitudes, and ideas. When minorities and women exercise positive thinking about getting a job, a great spiritual demonstration is required. The demonstration may be an exercise in which there are no readily available models to be visualized such as in the field of engineering.

There may be no role model to use for reassurance. By contrast, when a Caucasian thinks positively about getting a job, he or she can visualize successful models that are plentiful, and to whom there is easy access. Also, the minority person's career aspirations are held in check by the psychological barrier of being the "first" one. However, Caucasians can follow models of other Caucasians in high positions—i.e., the Presidency of the United States, which includes other Caucasians from George Washington to Ronald Reagan.

Researchers such as Parke Gibson and E. Franklin Frazier observed many differences in Blacks who used positive thought actions and those who did not.[8] Some of the differences found in Blacks with little or no practice in the use of positive thought action were:

- Blacks viewed themselves as being more manipulated in the work force than did Caucasians.[9] The same phenomenon was observed as a difference between men and women, in that women feel that things are done to them rather than their initiating actions.[10]

- Blacks behaved more passively than did Caucasians when preparing and presenting themselves in the work force. Blacks exhibited more thinking behaviors than doing, which reflected a lack of confidence.

- Blacks placed more value and emphasis on the effect of personal appearance and clothing than did Caucasians in the work force.

- Blacks spoke in more defensive tones, using the language of warfare to describe their jobs than did Caucasians. For instance, responding to how are you doing on your job, a Black might respond, "I'm just hanging on," or "I'm trying to see a little light at the end of the tunnel," or "I'm keeping out of the way of the heavy stuff," or "I can make it until my change comes." Caucasians might respond, "I'm involved in . . .," or "My boss seems to want me to . . .," or "My boss and I had a talk about . . .," or "I've applied for a new position as supervisor of . . ." [11]

Positive thinking, positive attitudes, and a positive action plan would change the responses of the minority and women workers to "I'm coping well," or "I'm a survivor," or "I win some and I lose some," or "I paid my phone bill and my car note by working today."

Observation of the factor race in the positive thinking process is a reminder that without a great deal of support Blacks often do excel because of their capacity for positive thinking. Jackie Robinson, William Warfield, and Booker T. Washington are examples of positive thinkers who overcame nearly insurmountable odds to be the first as well as the best in their endeavors.

The famous Black female educator Mary McLeod Bethune left a message that provides great clarity to the issue of race in positive thinking. Bethune said, "If a Black person sees a crack in the door of opportunity, they must put their head into the crack rather than their foot." Her legacy teaches us that we can do it, and we must do it. While Caucasians sacrifice one foot to succeed, minorities and women sometimes must be willing to sacrifice their heads.

Racism and sexism ran rampant over Mary McLeod Bethune and her peers in the early 1900's. She persevered, she called for help, she reached out to others. She used the tools of integrity, self-determination, positive thinking and actions to make her dream of a school — Bethune-Cookman College for Black Women — come true.

The unrelenting permanence of the two phenomena, racism and sexism, is almost unbelievable. *Racism* is defined as any action, attitude, or institutional structure that subordinates one group to another on the basis of race. *Sexism* is the act of subordinating a group or withholding rights and/or privileges from a group on the basis of sex. The permanence of the subordination that occurs is always hard to deal with.

In the world of work both racism and sexism affect the lives and jobs of both minorities and women. Coping with racism and sexism on the job involves the ability to identify and to acknowledge the real issues. Dr. Meg Wheatley from Goodmeasure, Inc., an organizational consulting firm, has determined that the issues affecting your ability to deal with racism and sexism are how to develop alliances, how to view the job as a building block, and how to view your critical job activities based on your level of authority.[12]

Wheatley cautions against the much lauded single mentor relationship. Since sponsors and mentors provide coaching, counseling, backup, endorsement, and information, you will need to identify several people who are willing to contribute to your job success.[13]

The development of several mentors requires time, patience, and the vision of an opportunist. For example, several months may be needed in order to accompany a manager from another department to a meeting where she can hear you make a presentation, thereby developing an interest in you as a worker. The *building block theory* has the positive aspects not included in the *stepping stone theory*. When the problems indigenous to racism and sexism in the work force occur, most often we invoke the stepping stone theory. We sometimes only investigate the answers to questions such as, "How do I make certain not to become marooned here with the bigoted or chauvinistic boss?" or "How do I avoid the dead-endedness of this job that has only been held by other minority persons?"

By contrast, if using the building block theory, the questions would become, "How can I perform so that I am noticed and the organization is rewarded?" or "How can I attract the attention of the right people?" A successful career can be built where there is institutional racism and sexism. If you were to examine and to acquire those skills and knowledge that you needed to do the job, you would be forced to explore the kinds of tasks that would highlight your professional competencies. Also, you would engage those people in relationships that would provide positive professional feedback and support.

Since society is so sharply focused on issues that could threaten the traditional power base of the majority population, it is highly unlikely that organizations and institutions will address the challenges that face minorities and women in the work force. The problems of minority persons in the work force, then, must be directed by individual commitments and action plans.

Expectations
in the Real World of Work

CHAPTER TWO

CHAPTER TWO

"The workplace has long been dominated by the rule of the carrot and the stick—as if we were a nation of donkeys. But the carrot—the lure of material well-being as defined by money and possessions—is subtly losing its savor. And the stick—once a brutal club labelled 'economic insecurity'—has thinned down to a flaccid bundle of twigs."
— *Daniel Yankelovich*
"The Meaning of Work"

Expectations in the Real World of Work

Minorities and women in the work force constantly face a world of decisions, tasks, and choices that involve accomplishments, and more importantly, their mere survival on jobs. *Job* is defined by Webster as any undertaking or employment with a view to profit, or any definite piece of work. A job usually is the result of a chosen vocation for which one has been specifically trained. Jobs lead to careers in which people seek to advance, to progress, and to move rapidly in their professions or jobs. Careers require the discharge of the objectives and official duties of the job.

Careering may provide social esteem if the worker is "on track" or upwardly mobile, that is, advancing at the expected pace. Traditionally, in the literature on career patterns, choices, and job selection, workers were advised to respond to the carrots, money, and career advancement as priorities for decision making. Minorities and women workers were cautioned to avoid accepting jobs that could be dead-ended positions, that were considered lower status positions, that promised lower pay, or jobs that were for blue collar workers.

Minorities and women have found that surviving in the real world of work requires a totally different approach. The definitions, assumptions, purposes, and characteristics of the real world of work set the stage on which these workers act. We must understand some concepts of work and the framework in which jobs operate. We must determine the nature of work, the scope of the job, and the development of careers in order to have sufficient tools for survival.

Work is defined by Webster as an effort directed to an end, employment, or the act of producing, achieving, or attaining something. Psychological literature has described the need to do meaningful work as an important part of the needs system of average Americans. Black workers have a history that dates back to ancient African civilizations that shows that people, families, and tribes were defined by their craft or work. African civilizations did not place the same social values on the same work areas that we see in present day society. However, great value was placed on the ability to do meaningful work. Such value was essential to the preservation of the social, psychological, and economic fibre of the people.

The famous French author, Count Alexis de Tocqueville, wrote about two observations that he made about the world of work during slavery in America. De Tocqueville wrote about the system of class in Europe separating Caucasians based on some being rich while others were poor. In America, de Tocqueville observed that Caucasians were united in the concept which considered all whites equal and held that Caucasians were superior to Blacks and over Blacks. Secondly, de Tocqueville concluded that as a result of the proliferation of slave labor, Caucasians regarded all labor as a sign of inferiority. [14] Such logic led to a sequence of ideas that said, slaves work, so work is to be shunned, since slaves are to be shunned.

The lure of career advancement in white collar jobs as a carrot for all Americans can be traced to the habits and prejudices of American colonists. The mint-julep aristocrats, and the charming and neurotic Caucasian ladies of the big houses, the fun of the hunt, the idleness, the pretensions to sophistication can be found today in the trappings of organizational behavior and corporate structure. Is the three martini lunch but a distorted version of the mint-julep aristocrat? Is the Caucasian female who decides that she is willing to compromise away her time, her dreams, her needs for the privilege of wearing a white shirt and navy suit not closely related to the charming lady of the plantation veranda? What, then, was the logic for and the chance of success of the minority workers during Jefferson's time as compared to minority workers in the 1980's?

Work as a social system has persevered and has preserved many of the components of racism and sexism. It is essential that minorities and women examine their roles, goals, and expectations related to work. In the words of the philosopher Santayana, "those who ignore history are condemned to repeat it." Conclusions drawn from an investigation of the real world of work must include an historical, as well as a present day review of trends in the workplace.

Black Americans have always worked because there was never a choice if they were to survive. The early Black worker performed slave labor without pay, but for the same purpose—in order to survive.

U.S. Bureau of the Census statistics show the median incomes of Black workers to be significantly below that of Caucasian workers. For example, in the category of workers who have one to three years of college, median income for the Caucasian husband is $15,722 and his wife $9,466. By comparison, median income for the Black husband would be $13,312 and his wife would earn $9,398. Together the Caucasian couple would earn $25,188 and the combined income for the Black couple would be $22,710.[15] Closer examination of other Bureau of Census statistics lead to the following three important and inescapable conclusions:

1. Within each race and sex category, even though there are large race and sex differences in income, without exception, the rule is: the higher the education level, the higher the median annual income;

2. Caucasian males at all educational levels have larger mean annual incomes than Black males;

3. Income differentials between the sexes are much greater than between Caucasians and Blacks at every educational level, even when the level of educational attainment is the same. The subtle factors related to differences in socialization, education and occupational expectations, and the operation of labor markets, tend to continue to reinforce discriminatory trends and practices. Therefore, minorities and women in America face gaps in earnings that amount to continued underpayment.

The challenge for minorities and women is to use tools for survival in order to gain resources to meet our human needs even when the labor force is fraught with the results of racism and sexism and the debilitating effects of discrimination. A secondary challenge is to be able to function knowing that any changes in these conditions will come in tiny increments and may have a very temporary effect. A good example of this is shown in recent reports on the state of the concept of voluntary affirmative action as decided by the Weber vs.

Kaiser Aluminum case and predictions of changes in that decision asked for by the Reagan Administration.

The Women's Movement of the 1970's saw few Black women participate. Some attention has been given to the question of the wisdom of Black women who did not eagerly join or participate in the movement. Caucasin females saw as a goal their label of homemaker. Black females had never had the nest syndrome as the majority of Black females had always worked. In the early urbanization of America, Black males went off to the military, served as porters on trains, and acted as laborers in the building trades. Black females worked to supplement their incomes and cared for families alone because the jobs took the men away from home for long periods of time.

The Women's Movement had little appeal to the Black female, who knew that corporate America was not waiting for her to darken its doorstep. Other cultural traditions were violated by the notion that to be liberated meant bra burning and sexual promiscuity. Sociologists had already portrayed the Black female as a promiscuous person who did not like to work. So to join such a movement would have fulfilled all of the myths held by and promoted by the dominant society.

Black females also express concern that they see the enemy in the fight against racism and sexism as the Caucasian male. That man is the father, son, brother, uncle, cousin, classmate, friend or husband of Caucasian females. Therefore any coalition formed to fight Caucasians could not be honest or very effective if Blacks joined Caucasians. The question became, Is water thicker than blood or vice versa? The answer as seen in the results of Affirmative Action in America is that the old adage is correct: "Blood is thicker than water." Caucasian females improved their salaries to the point that their problems shifted from equal pay for equal *work* to equal pay for comparable *worth*. The Black female is still seeking representation and participation. She still serves as token and often sacrificial lamb in the workplace.

Discussions of the problems that challenge minorities and women in the workforce result in strong negative feelings and nagging doubt about surviving. We should examine some things to do and some answers to the basic survival questions, such as:

1. Do minority workers have realistic perceptions and expecta-

tions of job requirements?
2. What constitutes success for minority workers?
3. What are some factors that ensure job security for minority workers?
4. What are the advantages and disadvantages of career choices in white vs. blue collar jobs for minority workers?
5. What are the characteristics of the world of work that relate directly to the survival of the minority worker?

The location of the job, type of job, salary, opportunity for advancement, and nature of the work are all important factors to be considered in career choice decisions. However, statistics on chronic diseases and actuary charts on life expectancy for Caucasians and Blacks provide information that should be used for understanding the world of work.

The benefits of the world of work accrue only to those who live to collect wages and pensions while in good health. The high rate of heart disease, hypertension, diabetes, and some forms of cancer among Black workers alerts us that some consideration of health hazards and levels of stress must also become a part of career choice decisions. As the Orwellian 1984 approaches, minorities and women should ask some of the following questions:

1. What can I do to gain resources to take care of my needs?
2. What am I willing to invest to do this job?
3. What kinds of dues am I willing to pay?
4. How many of my principles am I prepared to compromise?
5. How does this job relate to my personal need and reward systems?

Minorities and women are asked for proof of their qualifications and skills. Caucasian males are viewed in terms of their potential for growth and skills development. Minorities and women must know ways to sell the evidence of their marketable skills and their hard earned experiences. Some prospective employers are buying evidence of the following employee traits:

1. Willlingness to learn a new skill;
2. Willingness to foster positive interpersonal relations;
3. Willingness to work with others;

4. Willingness to exchange a day of labor for a day's pay.

William Raspberry reported in his article "Job Expectations Are Unrealistic" that many Black workers appear arrogant, lazy, and to lack ambition because they talk about jobs only in terms of how the job can benefit them and what they feel they have coming from the job. Raspberry reports that such attitudes cause Blacks to respond to interview questions in terms of the job being a conduit for delivering money to people, for how they want to live, and for how they want to dress. The problem, states Raspberry, is that Blacks often have no sense of what work really is about in American institutions and organizations. [16]

Raspberry feels that Blacks become separated from reality by living in homes where income means a welfare check, unrelated to any form of labor or work, or job programs that emphasize the needs of the unemployed rather than their abilities to produce or to perform something of value to the employer. There is also the problem of work that doesn't look like work.

There is great disjunction between receipt of a paycheck and producing something of value for Blacks who observe the salaries of professional athletes and people in entertainment. Lawyers, consultants, and executives disappear in board and conference rooms, have a generous and expensive lunch, and do not seem to the Black observer to have provided any service or to have produced anything of value. Learning about the world of work takes observation, experience, discussion, guidance, and patience.

Dr. Adele M. Scheele in a speech entitled "Women on the Move" told the audience that the workplace is filled with two kinds of workers, namely, sustainers and achievers. Scheele says that sustainers are the workers who do what they are told and wait for praise and recognition to come their way. Achievers accomplish tasks and demonstrate excellence in their performance consistently. Achievers "toot their own horns" and talk about their accomplishments. They are recognized, awarded, and rewarded for their professional efforts. They build these connections into their work tasks. The salaries of achievers grow steadily as they gain trust and acceptance of their efforts.

#7 **TOOL FOR SURVIVAL**

Do not assume that either a high school diploma or a college degree in any field whatever represents a cashier's check for a rewarding job and a decent income.

Study, analyze, and question your expectations and the job market to determine what the real world of work means to you. If you need to know more, keep asking—look, listen, and learn.

Examine your attitudes as you do some reality testing.

Test reality by using questions from your own personal needs system.

During the 80's you will need to use chutzpah, realism, and a high sense of self-interest in order to survive. [17]

Redefining Success and Security

In the world of work, minorities and women have been diagnosed as having at least 500 different kinds of the blues. Blues could be defined as day-to-day disappointments. People try to find vehicles for success and security. When people do not find solutions to problems that threaten security and success, they are candidates for the blues. Traditionally, people worked for success and job security based on the carrot theory, in which salaries were dangled as the magnet that attracted their labors.

More money, upward mobility, and advancement were sought after and were sold as certified tickets to success and job security. Workers who were "on track" were thought to have assurances of success and job security and were further thought to be immune to attacks of the blues.

Recent research on stress and career burnout shows us that reduction in force is no longer restricted to minorities and females.

Reduction in force, sometimes called rifting, has caused workers to begin to redefine success and job security. Caucasian workers in the insurance companies, government agencies, and the auto industry found that not having jobs as a result of rifting could happen after many years of diligence and hard work. Dedicated employees found that organizations no longer "looked after" their peole. Workers found that no matter how large the corporation was it could be turned upsidedown in this age of "Rollover" dollars. When organizations get into trouble in the 80's, they do not hesitate to get rid of even their oldest and most loyal employees. The top executives who made the decisions that caused the disaster continue to earn six-figure salaries and to make noises about policy changes and changes in program focus while other employees seek survival.

Minorities and women survived the forties when they were told that they had served but were no longer needed. Blacks survived the sixties when to be Black meant that Caucasians questioned why Blacks had not pulled themselves up by their bootstraps. Women and minorities survived the seventies, which was a time of wait-and-see, and a time taken by Caucasians to discuss whether or not further desegregation programs and affirmative action were really needed. Black survival in the eighties will not come from chants of "Black is Beautiful," "Black Power," "Burn Baby Burn," or "We Shall Overcome." Minorities and women who survive the eighties will be those who demonstrate quick thinking, who exhibit a keen sense of competition, and who use basic survival instincts to gain employment and to turn their salaries into statements of economic independence.

Success was once defined as expensive clothes and glamorous vacations. For others, success was the ability to owe a huge mortgage on a home, to owe installment payments on a car that cost more than food, and to owe installment payments on a car that cost more than food, and to owe huge balances to American Express, MasterCard, and Visa.

Studies and articles show that minorities and women have begun to rethink the value and long term benefits of the trappings of success. Patricia O'Brien writes that more women than ever before opt for blue collar jobs. She says that the women who defined success as their title of executive assistant have found themselves still only one step above the secretarial pool. Now when secretaries look down from their office windows they discover women below them in hard hats working construction. [18]

Mary Lindenstein Walshok suggests that women are redefining success as evidenced by the following trends:

1. Women going into blue collar fields are three to four times greater in number than those going into law, medicine, and management.
2. Women have gained a far larger percentage of blue collar jobs since 1975 than they have in white collar fields.
3. Blue collar jobs result in more money and more independence.
4. Blue collar jobs are more challenging and more interesting than teaching, law, and the executive suite.
5. Jobs in the blue collar field are functional and have clear rules. [19]

Minority workers would do well to take a page from the book of blue collar women workers who gain from their work independence and clear-cut rules. Minority workers would be advised to ask themselves if the job would be interesting, functional, and challenging. Success for the Black worker could mean retraining for a vocational area where three to four times more minorities and women have gained entry. Booker T. Washington, founder of Tuskegee Institute, advocated that Blacks in America learn to read and to figure but that they always learn a trade for survival. W. E. B. DuBois felt that Black intellectuals and academicians were the key to the survival of the race. The 1980's leave little room to doubt that Black intellectuals are a new powerless class who have not solved the problems of the race and are themselves unemployed in large numbers.

Black professionals have tried politely to fit themselves into a world of work dominated by the subtle Caucasian male hierarchy. Black professionals are especially vulnerable during times of retrenchment and conservatism. Perhaps as Black workers redefine success and job security, they will add components such as a Booker T. Washington position supporting the acquisition of a technical and/or marketable skill in a trade. As the minority worker faces discrimination and harassment, knowledge of some blue collar field would allow a way to fight back and to be an aggressive survivor.

Blue collar jobs tend to be technical and service oriented. The heavy use of computers, information systems, and other technology

31

require that large numbers of people know how to service these products. Minorities and women have become entrepreneurs in the technical companies. Even though the American corporate uniform, the navy suit, white shirt, and tie, seem to set the benchmark for success, minorities and women workers may find success in blue collar jobs where they gain credit for their services. They are paid for service calls, and they experience satisfaction as they enjoy the non-ambiguous job atmosphere without strain and worry about office politics.

#8　　　　**TOOL FOR SURVIVAL**

Redefine success and job security using personal norms as criteria. Success for Black workers is being able to pass up prolonged stress, boredom, and the chore of incessantly trying to prove oneself worthy of the benevolent Caucasian who "allows" you to stay on the job. Success should be measured by the degree to which the Black worker benefits from a non-ambiguous job atmosphere, with concrete tasks, for which one receives out-on-the-table praise, independence, satisfaction, and visible proof of having performed a skilled labor. Job security means goodbye management studies, hello elevator mechanic class.

Getting the Job Done vs. The Hard Work Philosophy

How many workers have you heard discuss the idleness, lack of objectivity, and the pervasiveness of the Cover-Your-A_____ (Anatomy) rule perpetuated by Caucasian workers in the organization? Nearly everyone witnesses the reinforcement and reward system enjoyed especially in public sector jobs where calamitous flops are labeled just another bureaucratic foul-up rather than anyone's fault. Have you ever been called cold and heartless for pointing out errors in operation? Have you been accused of not being a team player when you reported an error made by another team member? Have you been ganged up on and made to look wrong as others cover up the blatant mistakes of a co-worker?

After cursory examination, the first answer seems to be that racism has again reared its ugly head. If the Black worker is also female, then the answer to "why me" seems to be that you are suffering from the whammy of the "two-fer" in the Caucasian, male dominated workforce. However, on closer examination you would find a third operational factor. That is, the politics of organizations require that you get the job done without rocking the boat. The truth behind this political requirement is that success in business requires much more than technical proficiency. So minimizing the amount of flack becomes more important than getting the job done.

Any person with experience in the world of work would advise you not to adopt the statement, "Hard work never hurt anyone." Hard work has often killed any chances for success or job security for Black workers. Public administration authors advise Black workers not to concentrate on their race and sex differences, but rather to think about strong bonds that they may share with Caucasian workers who have high professional standards and seek to make a valuable contribution to the organization. The fallacy in such advice is found in two documented phenomena:

1. Kanter sees—as a special condition facing tokens, women, and minorities—a situation called contrast and polarization. This special situation finds the dominant group perceiving and applying the race and sex role stereotypes which it has assigned to the subordinate group no matter how subordinate group members function. [20]

2. Korda states that hard work is not a prerequisite for survival in the workforce. Hard work tends to be seen as arrogant behavior. Hard workers are often alienated in the mainstream because they are viewed like the schoolroom pests who keep trying to prove themselves the smartest kids in the class. [21]

3. Many conscientious workers have had their careers derailed because they focused attention on completing the task while neglecting thoughts about the broader perspective of where the task fits within the objectives of the company.

Slow down. Get your nose away from the grindstone. Do not do your job so well that your volume of work changes the pace of the organization. When you get feedback that you appear to be an eager beaver, pull back. Assume a lower profile. Take a few days off to measure the accepted rate of other workers.

Polarization and contrast cause hard work on the part of a minority worker to be viewed by the dominant group without any understanding of the effort. The attention that such efforts would gain only serves to further alienate minority workers as they are felt not to be functioning "properly" within the assigned stereotypes. How often do minorities and women sit in a staff meeting, make a report, and gain negative feedback? Then, before the end of the meeting, the same idea, program, or suggestion is put before the group by a Caucasian worker and is approved or otherwise met with positive reactions. The minority worker often wonders, "Did they hear me?" "What do I have to do to gain credibility and recognition?"

The dominant group, using race and sex role stereotypes for thinking, does not hear. Nor will it ever provide the same reward or reinforcement for the efforts of the minority workers that it provides for its own. Minorities and women must remain flexible as they judge each situation to determine how much they must compromise in order to accommodate and to adapt to the system.

Ambitious employees must discover the underlying objectives and problems of the company in order to work within the constraints that emerge. Eager beavers seldom take their attention away from completing the work, but then they protest, "Why did you tell me to continue the work if you didn't really want the project?" Does that make sense? The right question is, "Where are the signs that this experimental project and innovation is compatible with the priorities of upper management."

#10 **TOOL FOR SURVIVAL**

The system for survival includes accommodation tactics, adaptation mechanisms, compromise strategies, and the illusion of graceful defeat.

Flexibility is the skill you experience using when you know you are in the flow. Flexibility means that change is an okay phenomenon.

Survival is an art. Survivors are artists. Survival must be learned as actors learn to act or as artists learn their craft. The most successful survivors are not found on the stage, but are found in everyday life. The best acting is not found on the stage, but in organizations and institutions.

Characteristics of the World of Work

Organizations in the American workforce are designed according to an historical hierarchy generally designating positions from the top levels and downward to line employees. The military hierarchy is the most graphic illustration of the design. The President of the United States is the Chief of the Armed Forces, the Pentagon houses top officers in all branches of the armed forces, and middle level officers are in charge of operations at military installations across the nation. There are numerous levels of officers down the ladder to the enlisted soldier. The functions, roles, responsibilities, and authority of *all* military personnel are predetermined, though the decisions and challenges that must be handled are constantly changing.

Analysis of the formal organizational structure reveals the following characteristics common to both the public and private sectors:

1. Hierarchy of authority, chain of command based on position;
2. Division of labor based on specialization of tasks;
3. Rules, regulations based on hierarchy and behavior norms;
4. Standardized procedures to handle major activities;
5. Specific purposes articulated in limited organizational objectives;
6. System of economic, material, and social rewards;
7. Communication systems both formal and informal;
8. Norms used as guidelines for acceptable and unacceptable behavior. [22]

Organizations have a specified purpose to achieve through coordinating the activities of human, financial, and natural resources. Organizations represent the means for accomplishing objectives set for a predetermined purpose. Traditionally, organizations in America have demonstrated more concern for organizational goals and survival than for the goals of individuals in their employ.[23] Therefore, the minority worker cannot survive without knowing the true purpose of the organization in which he or she works.

#11   TOOL FOR SURVIVAL

Know the *purpose* of the organization in which you are employed. Know the objectives of the organization. Know your task assignment clearly. Determine how your task assignment contributes to accomplishment of the organizational objectives.

All *formal* interaction within the organization occurs based on the established *hierarchy*. The hierarchy determines the position and relative authority exercised in each position of the organization. For example, the company owner and/or president represents the highest ranked decision-maker, and is therefore the top of the organization. The vice president represents the next level downward. The vice president is followed by department heads on the level below. The staff members are below department heads. Finally, line or support employees are on the bottom of the hierarchy.

The level of decision-making power is also determined by the hierarchy. The department heads have decision-making power, but it is subordinate to that of the company owner and/or president.

For example, the power and authority to make decisions about personnel recruitment may be designated exclusively to department heads. The company owner and/or president would not be concerned about such decisions at all. Conversely the company owner and/or president may have the exclusive decision-making power in acquiring new contracts for the firm.

The hierarchy determines the *chain of command* or formal lines of authority in the organization. The formal lines of *authority* explain to whom all employees are accountable, who is to supervise whom, and how employees communicate from the top of the pyramid to the bottom and vice versa.

The extent of power and authority generally increases as you go UP the hierarchy, and conversely, decreases as you move down the hierarchy. Communication generally travels downward from the most powerful at the top to lower levels. Responses or reports on completed projects travel upward to inform higher levels that organizational objectives have been met.

Organizations have established reward systems, which facilitate the distribution of financial, material, and social rewards. Workers receive financial compensation for task accomplishment in the form of wages, commission, or salaries predetermined as pay for each job or position.

Salaries are probably the most important factor in the development of a career. Higher salaried persons are those considered for expanded responsibilities and promotions. Career paths to upward mobility are strewn with green dollars. Women and minority workers face formidable obstacles as they struggle to gain equal pay for equal work as well as their battle for salaries representing pay for comparable worth.

Research and analyze, in detail, how your organization or agency is funded and supported. From the outside, the job may be one that enjoys prestige, a high degree of status, and respectability.

However, from the inside, the reality may be that the entire organization, agency, or division has no operational budget, may be totally dependent on outside funding sources, and the management strategies of the executives may be fraught with the insecurities and unpredictability of future funding.

Budgets are one of the most powerful forces in the organization.

This process is more clear-cut in the private sector (corporations and industry). There are significant exceptions to the rules for promotion and salary raises in the public sector: school districts, government agencies, and social programs. Minority workers in the public sector often are given enormous responsibilities in various areas, but are rarely compensated with promotions or salary increases. Minorities and women in the public sector are asked to "make sacrifices out of dedication to the client population: the disadvantaged." Phrases such as "it's just not in the budget" are often accepted by minority workers. It is assumed that work in the public sector is fulfilling the need to help those citizens of America as unfortunate as they themselves are. Studies show that minorities and women workers are overworked, grossly underpaid, and consistently denied promotions or raises in the public sector.

Material and social rewards function to reinforce behavior deemed acceptable for workers by the organization, and to punish unacceptable behavior by workers. Material rewards are items such as certificates of merit and achievement, cash bonuses, or special monthly recognition and trophies awarded to workers for work and/or behavior the organization supports. For example, many grocery store chains have a citywide selection of the Employee-of-the-Month based on job performance. The worker awarded this choice receives special recognition, photograph and announcement posted in the store, and possibly in the local newspaper.

Social rewards result generally from within the informal communication network, known as the grapevine, that develops in organizations. Positive or negative feedback about workers flows up and down the grapevine, from work group to management, and sometimes to top levels of the hierarchy. Social rewards may be a call to the manager's office for a "pat on the back" and spoken praise for a job well done, when positive feedback about a worker has reached the manager.

Workers who do not perform well, or who are not liked because they are perceived as different from their co-workers are victimized by the social reward system. Co-workers may generate negative feedback up the grapevine, which could result in a call to the manager's office to "be chewed out" by the manager for not cooperating with the team.

More often than not, minority workers find that negative feedback is their social reward no matter how well they perform their duties because they are perceived as different based on the societal stereotypes of the race/sex. Further discussion of this concept is detailed later in this Chapter in the Section "Team Building for Survival in the Workforce."

Minorities and women must function in the organization much like the foreigner with a different native language must operate in the dominant culture. They must understand and know the formal hierarchy, as well as rules and regulations. They must *also* be constantly aware that there is the old double standard that applies to them solely because they are minority workers. Betty Lehan Harragan reminds us of why minorities and women are victims of the double standard: "The existing system is the game of business . . . The rules of the game are those firmly established generations ago by the male WASP (White Anglo-Saxon Protestant) founders, whose descendants are still the star players." [24]

Organizations in the American workforce operate as mini-social systems within society exhibiting all the norms of the American society-at-large. Caucasian males dominate societal norm setting, and therefore also dominate the world of work. The accepted norms in American society perpetuate and encourage discrimination against minorities in the mainstream culture, and also in the workforce. Therefore minority and women workers must develop personal action plans to survive the discrimination in the workplace, as well as that found in the mainstream of American society.

Our true analysis and understanding of where power lies, who we are accountable to, and how our task completion contributes to the overall purpose of the organization must be based on *actual* and *real* characteristics of the organization. Minorities and women who follow the formal rules and regulations and honor the formal chain of command are not guaranteed survival within the organization.

Kanter observed that the determinants—proportion, opportunity, and power—greatly influence the behavior, and hence, the survival of minorities and women in the world of work. The following has been documented by Kanter about people whose type is represented in very small *proportion* in the workplace.

People low in proportion would tend to:

1. be more visible and be "on display";
2. feel more pressure to conform, to make fewer mistakes;
3. try to become "socially invisible," not to stand out so much;
4. find it harder to gain credibility, particularly in high uncertainty positions such as certain management jobs;
5. be more likely to be excluded from informal peer networks, and hence, limited in this source of power-through-alliances;
6. have fewer opportunities to be "sponsored" because of the rarity of people like them upward;
7. face misperceptions of their identity and role in the organization, and hence, develop a preference for already-established relationships;
8. be stereotyped, be placed in role traps that limit effectiveness;
9. face more personal stress. [25]

People low in *opportunity* would tend to:

1. limit their aspirations, not hoping for mobility in general, not valuing more responsibility, more participation;
2. have lower self-esteem, value their competence less than

adequately;

3. seek satisfaction in activities outside of work, dream of escape, and "interrupt" their careers (sometimes as a function of insecurity in the job itself);
4. be critical of high power people, of management, or at least, fail to identify with them;
5. but be less likely to protect directly or seek change; channel grievances into griping or restrict output rather than take direct action;
6. orient peer groups toward protection and reassurance, with strong loyalty demands, and hence, discourage members of the group from seeking mobility;
7. be more attached to the local unit than to the larger organization, and hence, be more parochial;
8. resign themselves to staying put;
9. be concerned with basic survival and extrinsic rewards: the the economic or social payoff of the job. [26]

People low in *organization power* would tend to:

1. foster lower group morale;
2. try to retain control, restrict opportunities for subordinates' growth or autonomy, supervise too closely;
3. use subordinates as their frame of reference for status assessment and enhancement;
4. try to hold back talented subordinates, thereby reducing the threat of replacement;
5. use more coercive than persuasive power;
6. be more insecure and thus more controlling, critical;
7. be very concerned about controlling a territory, and hang on to that territory, even when inappropriate;
8. be less well liked, less talkative in meetings with high power people. [27]

Persons low in proportion, Low in power, and low in opportunity who acquire and imitate negative, defensive behavior patterns have accepted feelings of inferiority and defeat in the world of work. These people are not survivors in the workforce, but seal their own doom by fulfilling the stereotype of workers who are "crabs in a bucket." Through negative behaviors, they not only hamper their own possibilities for career advancement and survival, but also contribute to the professional demise of fellow minority workers and talented minority subordinates. As the late Bob Marley sang, "When it rains, it don't rain on no one man's house." These people are tragic because they waste time, energy, and mental activity in negative behavior that results in alienation, dead-ended positions, and powerlessness in the work situation. Instead of dragging someone else back down into the bucket or holding on with claws so that no one moves, energies should be channeled to formulate a positive action plan so that more minority workers can be numbered with the "overcomers" in the world of work.

It is important to understand that minority workers who imitate these negative behaviors do so in predominantly white organizations, as well as in the rare all-minority staff organizations. Interestingly, organizations with all-Black staffs also operate as mini-social systems in which Blacks parrot the self-defeatist, oppressive mentality of "Plantation Politics" like many Black Americans in the mainstream. Studies of oppression conclude that the oppressed eventually accept and believe what the oppressor defines them to be.[29] Sadly, Black Americans who accept inferiority, second-class citizenship, and the "less than human" roles that the oppressor has assigned to them, live very non-productive lives. Minority workers who accept these norms are sometimes very oppressive of other minority workers in the world of work.

Minorities and women must become aware of behaviors in the work situation that gain positive results for those who survive. Kanter provides an extensive description of more positive behaviors based on the same determinants: proportion, opportunity, and power.

People whose type is represented in *very high proportion* would tend to:
1. be easily seen as one of the group, as fitting in;
2. be preferred for high-communication managerial jobs;
3. find it easier to gain "credibility" for high uncertainty positions, such as some management jobs;
4. be more likely to join the informal network, form peer alliances, learn the ropes from peers;
5. be accurately perceived, have a congruent identity, and ease in self-presentation;

7. face less personal stress.

People *high* in *opportunity* would tend to:

1. have high aspirations;
2. have high self-esteem, value or overrate their competence;
3. consider work a more central life interest;
4. be more committed to the organization, willing to sacrifice for it and believe in its goals;
5. be competitive, oriented toward rivalry;
6. be more attracted to high power people, seek validation from, identify with them;
7. create power- and action-oriented informal groups;
8. when dissatisfied, engage in active change-oriented forms of protest: collective action, formal meetings, suggestions for change;
9. consider themselves members of the larger organization rather than the local unit;
10. be concerned with the job as an instrument for mobility and growth, and hence, with intrinsic aspects such as its potential for learning.

People *high* in *organizational power*:

1. foster high group morale;
2. have subordinates who inhibit their negativity and aggressiveness, behaving in more cooperative and less critical ways, thereby reducing the need to exercise strong controls;
3. behave in less rigid, directive, authoritarian ways, to delegate more control and allow subordinates more latitude and discretion;
4. provide opportunities for subordinates to move along with them, find talented subordinates and groom them for better things;
5. have their actions seen more often as helping than hindering;
6. be better liked, talk more often, and receive more communications in meetings.

During the 1970's, major corporations began to hire token numbers of women. Ten years later women have made impressive progress at the entry level and in mid-level management positions. However, large numbers of women and men report discrimination as the major problem for women who try to break into positions in senior management. 117 of 300 women executives polled by UCLA's Graduate School of Management and Korn/Ferry International felt that being a woman was the greatest obstacle to their success. [28]

Research by Ann Harlan and Carol Weiss suggests that the degree, level and condition of the discrimination does not necessarily improve as the number of women in the organization increases. Their Wellesley College Center research from 1982 challenges the theory advanced by experts who held that as an organization attained a critical mass of executive women somewhere between 30% and 35%, job discrimination would vanish. In a three year study, Harlan and Weiss found that while overt resistance drops quickly after the first few women become managers, it increases as the number of women reaches 15%. In a study of two companies where the first had only 6% of women as managers, and the second with 19%, more women in the second company complained of discrimination than did women from the smaller group of managers. [29]

Team Building for Survival in the Workplace

There are many barriers to the development of belongingness skills which support team concepts in the world of work. Social customs, cultural differences, and old assumptions about acceptable team building and team membership in organizations build barriers between Caucasians and minorities in the workforce. Some barriers derive from prejudices and stereotypes found in habits, thoughts, hidden agendas, and the very nature of the settlement of America. The barriers are unique in that they satisfy a social environment associated with Caucasian male preferences, habits, and symbols.

These barriers undermine possible bonding of Black and Caucasian workers who attempt such tasks as concrete thinking, delegating authority, development of control, command, trust, understanding, good will, and self-confidence. The barriers make it difficult for minorities and women to engage in successful team building, and to adopt the effective subtleties which earn team membership. Barriers to team building skills and team membership must be overcome in order to properly develop the competence and the ambitions of the minority and majority workers.

One of the pervasive myths related to team building is that women and other minorities can function effectively as tokens within organizations. However, according to Rosabeth Moss Kanter, tokens face special situations based on how tokens are perceived. Kanter proposes that while X's represent the Caucasian male in the workforce, then O's represent minorities and women, and,

". . . . if one sees nine X's and one O

X X X
X XOX
X XX

the O will stand out. The O may also be overlooked, but if it is seen at all, it will get more notice than any X. Further, the X's may seem more alike than different because of their contrast with the O."[30]

Kanter's research documents that there are three perceptual tendencies regarding the proportional rarity of tokens which operate as factors in organizations. Any set of objects is perceived based on: *visibility, contrast,* and *assimilation.* The factors generate special pressures for minority workers. First tokens are highly *visible* and gain attention. Tokens are more highly visible than the dominants when looked at alone, and capture a higher level of awareness. Tokens fulfill the "law of increasing returns," in that:

> "... as individuals of their type represent a small numerical proportion of the overall group, they each potentially capture a larger share of the awareness given to that group,"

The second perceptual tendency about tokens is known as *contrast* or polarization of differences. In uniform groups, common culture may be taken for granted. However, the presence of a person or two who has a different set of social characteristics increases the self-consciousness of the dominant group. The most damaging behavior occurs as the dominant group tends to exaggerate the extent of the differences between groups. The token is then isolated because of the heightened focus on the dominant culture boundaries.[31] The boundaries are set in order to preserve the commonalities of the dominant culture and to push the token outside and to retain the differences of the token. For example, contrast might appear as in this diagram:

```
X   X   X                    O
  X   X
X   X   X                    O
```

The third perception of tokens shows that tokens are more easily stereotyped than are people found in the greater proportion. This perception is called *assimilation* and involves the use of sterotypes and the characteristics of a token being distorted to fit some familiar generalization about a person's social type. Since it is easy for tokens to find an identity by conforming to a stereotype, few discrepant examples occur. So tokens are highly visible as "different" and yet are not permitted the individuality of their own unique non-stereotypical characteristics.[31]   As an example assimilation might resemble this diagram:

46

	X-ness	O-ness
X X X	X	O
X X	X	O-
X	X	O_x

Assimilation involves the use of stereotypes to generalize about a particular social type. Tokens suffer two ways as assimilation operates:

1. Tokens are more easily stereotyped than are members of the dominant culture; and
2. Tokens are highly visible as people who are different and are not perceived as acting in any individual or unique, non-stereotypical way.

Taylor and Fisher studied impressions of subjects to groups. The picture illustrations included an all Caucasian male group and an all Caucasian male with one Black male group. Disproportionate attention was paid to the token. The token was perceived as playing some highly stereotypical role. Also, by contrast, in integrated groups, subjects' recollections were the same for Caucasians and Blacks.[32] The researchers demonstrated the difficulties experienced as minority workers seek any state of belongingness within organizations. Team building skills help to create a feeling of ease with colleagues.

Frederick Douglass wrote that,

"the negro be not judged by the heights to which he is risen, but by the depths from which he has climbed."

Using such an evaluation criterion, minorities and women who survive in the workforce are modern day miracle workers.

Rosabeth Moss Kanter acknowledges the dilemma faced by minorities and women in organizations as they face racism in the Goodmeasure, Inc. training film, "The Tale of O." Kanter describes the X's as members of the majority population and O's as minorities and women. The film shows the behaviors of O's as they seek to gain success on the job. The O's resort to behaviors characterized by:

1. Rebellion against X's shown by O's staying to themselves.
2. Attempts to assimilate shown by O's denigrating themselves through humor to please the X's.

3. Attempts at assimilation based on the efforts used by O's to show how much they really look like X's.
4. Attempts made by O's to bring little or no attention to themselves so that they become lost in a crowd of X's.

Since society is so sharply focused on issues that could threaten the traditional power base of the majority population, it is highly unlikely that organizations and institutions will address the challenges that face minorities and women in the work force. The problems of minority persons in the work force, then, must be directed by individual commitments and action plans.

Tokenism is defined for minorities and women as being a mere symbol or semblance, rather than an identifiable and effective reality. In organizations tokens and minority workers are counted in statistics, appear on payrolls, are present while not really counting needed employees, and are not known as people. It is not the currents of tokenism in themselves that cause problems for minorities and women. The problems arise when the real meaning of tokenism cannot be put aside at inappropriate moments, and when tokenism is used as a proxy for power. Such power brokering raises the level of ambivalence of minority workers, and reduces their ability to feel comfortable with their colleagues and the ability to be equal companions at work. Clarity takes the place of ambivalence when individuals are able to interpret their own roles.

Experience, power, and expertise all help minorities and women to feel less self-conscious in organizations. Integrated organizations which have large numbers of minority workers have assuaged the problems faced by tokens in the workforce. Since there is still a great deal of skepticism about the skills and talents of minority workers, minorities and women who already have a foothold in an organization may have to intercede on behalf of others. Part of the role of the established minority worker may be to instruct up-and-coming minorities and women. They may need to orient the new workers by talking to them about business and informal expectations.

Every minority and woman worker that you know, friend or foe, goes through traumatic, hurtful, job-related problems.

When you examine a situation and begin to feel defeated, dejected, denigrated, denounced, and devalued, sit down and make a list of ten of your minority friends. Under each name jot down disappointments and setbacks that each suffered during the past two years on the job. Then look for the similarities between your predicament and things that your friends have lived through. In the margin of your list note how long each situation lasted. Pray for patience and endurance.

You, too, will overcome this difficulty. It only takes one retirement, one promotion, or one of any other type of hierarchal or structural change to have a new set of factors with which to deal, or to change your problem to an opportunity.

We must examine the development of skills that ensure successful team membership and employment patterns. Any system within an organization would involve skills development for team building among faculty, staff, support, professional, and supervisory personnel. The skills found in the system would have three similarities:

1. Effective use of the system requires improving communications;
2. Making adequate connections within the organization and environmental management; and
3. Development of team building skills in order to facilitate planning, organization, directing, coordinating, reporting, and budgeting.

Any approach to skills development would only be as successful as the implementation process adopted by the employers and the employees. Skills could be developed in an implementation process that included the following areas:

I. IMPROVEMENT OF COMMUNICATIONS
   A. Improvement of self-image.
   B. Improvement of image of agency, organization and/or field of endeavor.
   C. Development of public relations background and understandings.
   D. Utilization of system-wide communications linkages that ensure feedback, input, and output.

II. CONNECTIONS WITHIN THE ORGANIZATION
   A. Establishing credibility based on skill and knowledge.
   B. Developing up-to-date, validated, human and professional resources.
   C. Identifying the formal and informal dynamics within the system for the purpose of team building.
   D. Accomplishing team building skills through networking.

III. ENVIRONMENTAL MANAGEMENT FOR TEAM BUILDING
   A. Improvement of program development, design, scope, and content.
   B. Modifying the work environment in order to accommodate and cooperate with significant others.
   C. Establishing time-management goals.
   D. Utilization of a delivery system of services that has an accountability scheme responsive to clients.
   E. Modification of the work environment to enhance the quality of worklife and productivity of the worker.

IV. CORPORATE CULTURE ASSESSMENT
   A. The shaping of corporate values and purposes.
   B. Corporate culture dominance and coherence.
   C. Pervasive corporate legends, parables, networks, and philosophies.

#15   TOOL FOR SURVIVAL

It is helpful to have a concerned minority or woman worker to provide support and encouragement. This tool really guides you to seek team membership wherever you find that you share the same interests.

Team membership may become a reality through identifiable stages of development. The following outline shows the stages moved through while the individual attempts team building in an organization.

Stage I. CANDIDATE

When you are in trouble or need help, others will not come to your assistance if you are only a *candidate* for team membership.

Operational factors for O's:
1. Small network develops with little or no assistance available.
2. Candidate is observed by leader.
3. Candidate is considered for team membership.

State II. FINALIST

When you are a *finalist*, one of the ways that you earn team membership is to have the leader and other members make a commitment to view you as a team player.

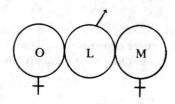

O = Minority worker
M = Team member
L = Team leader

Operational factors for O's:
1. Commitment to you develops.
2. Others acknowledge your capabilities.
3. You may function one step above candidate as a finalist.
4. You may function without clear-cut tasks and responsibilities.

Team membership is granted by others. Team membership is a privilege that is bestowed upon you, not a right that one can gain.

Workers must know and understand that their team building can be short-circuited in any of the four stages. Workers may be caught for long periods in any one of the four stages. So patience and the ability to watch-and-wait may be a much needed skill.

Stage III. TEAM MEMBER

When you function as a *team member* you actually work on organizational goals as a result of the approval of particular team members.

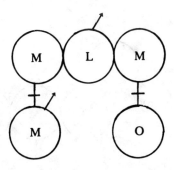

Operational factors for O's:
  1. Approval is gained from leaders.
  2. More benefits are received from leader and members.
  3. O's begin to function with clear-cut tasks and responsibilities.

#18 **TOOL FOR SURVIVAL**

Teams are informed organizations. Any member must be cautioned that the rules of the team may be even more restrictive than those announced by the parent organization.

The team rules, though almost never written, must be followed by members. Be prepared for possible rule changes that may develop as a result of political or structural changes from outside the team itself.

Stage IV. SELECTED TEAM MEMBER

As a *selected team member,* you have been accepted into an elite group. You may stay as long as the rules and regulations of this privileged class are observed.

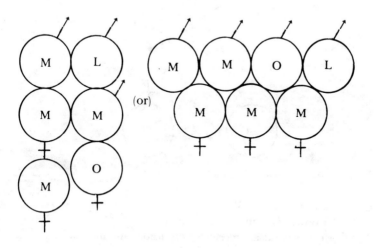

Operational factors for O's:
1. O's may sometimes function as leader.
2. O's become a member of a class with special protection.
3. O's may become a power broker.
4. O's gain recognition and accolades that have been acquired by the group.
5. O's function with clearly defined tasks and responsibilities accompanied by authority.

#19   **TOOL FOR SURVIVAL**

Only after Stage IV — Selected Team Member, can you assume that your team membership provides you protection and gives you security. It is only in Stage IV that you may learn those rules which allow you to retain your team membership. All protections given are contingent upon your continued acceptable behavior.

Prepare and Present Yourself

CHAPTER THREE

CHAPTER THREE

Preparation is rarely easy and never beautiful.
Maya Angelou — Singin' and Swingin' and Makin' Merry
Like Christmas

Prepare and Present Yourself

The games of power and politics that formulate the environment in the world of work often present serious problems and real barriers for workers. Often the power and political games form a nebulous cloud over the work life. The key question to developing career prowess is to ask their personal advantage? The purpose for pursuing answers to the question is to discover tools for survival that reward persons who want to get along and to get ahead in the jobs.

This chapter will introduce the reader to skills that are not traditionally taught in schools. These skills are sometimes thought to be innate or other times thought to be gained through the trial and error process. Both processes happen for some individuals. However, minority and women workers who may not survive long enough to experience the results of trial and error must arm themselves in the workforce. These are behavioral skills that have valuable crossover and transferability to many careers no matter what the career content.

HOW TO PREPARE YOURSELF

The cultural traditions of Black workers passed along from the time of slavery in America elevated hard work to an undeserved and dangerous pedestal. An action plan based on "I'll just do my job and stay out of the politics" has contributed to the career burnout and the eventual demise of too many minority and women workers. Though there is little justification for a job well done taking second or third place to getting along with others and getting ahead, the most lucrative rewards have not been gained for hard work. Noses to the grindstone, hearts filled with commitment, and faces beaming with good intentions come face-to-face with the parade of power seekers, power brokers, and political manueverers, who pass by in a rush of wind that drowns out the career plans of persons who have dedicated all of their energies only to getting the job done.

Adele Scheele asserts that successful workers are those who make visible a hidden curriculum filled with sets of careering skills that may be considered illegitimate by colleges and universities. [32] One set of careering skills is called *connecting skills*. Connecting skills are those which allow you to use your college, mentor, research, internship, and apprenticeship experiences to assist you to meet your employment goals. Connecting skills promote links with mentors, colleagues, managers, and faculty to build bridges to the business and professional experiences that you need to survive in the world of work and to make a living. For example, if a supervisor suggests that anyone at the next level up will have to possess a certain technical skill to move up, you must find apprenticeships, internships and training seminars that will fulfill the requirement. Sometimes, a lateral transfer within the organization can be a profitable one because of the new connecting skills potential.

Scheele describes six critical career competences present in the successful careers that she analyzed. Though these critical career competences were derived from the ethnomethodological study of lawyers, there is great crossover and transfer potential for Black workers.

Scheele delineates each of the critical career competences as teachable. Each career competency requires both concept formation and the developmental process for successful completion. Each of the critical career competences has first developmental levels, which refers to their endless capacity for improvement which is measurable only in progressive stages. Secondly, each competence has a sequential level, which refers to the capacity for building on and leading to the next process and skill. [33]

BUILDING CONNECTING SKILLS

A sense of personal power must be perceived in order to acquire the first two skills. They are skills which, when gained, demonstrate personal courage. The skills that build connections and personal courage for career success are:

1. *Experiencing doing* means a combination of recognizing one's likes and dislikes of the doing, as well as the performing of an independent action. For example, experiencing doing is a way of knowing and confirming one's own world of actions, reactions, and assessments. [34] You could ask questions about how you feel while you are performing a work task. Traditionally, we only ask how we feel after performing a task. A clear statement about likes and dislikes cannot emerge if one is only getting through or completing the task. We must learn to check out feelings during the process and the experiencing of the doing.

#20   **TOOL FOR SURVIVAL**

Play the hand that is dealt to you. Identify what you must discard as well as what you must keep. Play the hand as best you can. Do not wait on another hand and do not pass.

Use even failure as information. Failure only means that one card did not turn a trick. A lost trick does not mean that you are not a skilled player. If you lose the bid, go down gracefully and calmly, and quietly analyze what happened. Get ready for the next hand.

---

2. *Risk linking* is an open statement that demonstrates a willingness to chance connections. This skill is not a gamble in a win/lose game. Risk linking means that you are willing to connect in order to experience ideas, styles, and organizations with other individuals. The risks in linking are related to the process of satisfying curiosity and exploring in the world of work. Risk linking does not mean that you suspend the use of good judgments or strong intuitions. Risk linking means to carry out experiments in which you select what to risk, and where to risk while exploring both concrete and abstract relationships. [35] Risk linking makes for legitimate exploration and experimentation with associates, relationships, styles of behavior,

and non-traditional ways of thinking.

The practice of risk linking may make you experience either dissonance or receptivity. Risk linking is the test used to find out the potential practicality and suitability of a consideration. Minority workers should take time to apply social and cultural traditions such as putting the ear to the ground, listening to nature throb and interpreting the beat of the drums. The product of the minority worker's analysis of the connections heard, seen, felt, and sensed should be used. The resulting data from risk linking may instruct the worker to willingly leave the situation, to set him/herself apart from the relationship, or to further explore the situation. Whichever decision that results should only be labeled *change*, not failure or differences, not deviations. [36]

BUILDING BEHAVIORAL SKILLS

The second two skills have to do with organizational behavior. They are the skills for *displaying belongingness* and for *exhibiting specializing*.

3. Displaying belongingness is the act of confirming affiliation with a group by demonstration. Scheele says further that showing belongingness is comprised of actions by the individual toward the group in order to assert membership. Belonging, then, is an essential process that begins with an invitation or request to join the group. [37]

This skill is perhaps the most elusive of all of the critical career competencies for minority workers to develop. If the formation of groups and teams begins with an invitation or a request, one may be delayed and the other deferred because of the lack of an adequate communications network.

Minorities' and women workers' past associations and their socialization patterns tend to be different from those of the Caucasian and dominant culture groups. For example, a Black worker may have contacts in the Urban League, the NAACP, Black sororities and fraternities, and other groups that have a majority membership of Black persons. Even as a student in a predominantly

Caucasian university, the social activities and other interests of Black students may be quite different from Caucasian students. Therefore, in the pre-professional stage, the Black worker might attend conferences and conventions that provided information and support for the Black worker. Even when both workers attend the same convention, they will select different meeting tracks. Consequently, by the time the Black worker seeks team membership and a collaborative mode in the workplace, often the only thing that the Black worker and the Caucasian worker have in common is the job.

Showing belongingness is a very subtle and nearly invisible skill. Yet, it is most essential as one must belong in order to maintain membership in an organization. The most skillful demonstration of showing belongingness is to act in ways that are non-threatening and that cause the least flack to the group. Rosabeth Moss Kanter's studies show that the mere color of the skin causes the dominant culture, Caucasians, to become self-conscious and uncomfortable when there are few minorities and women. Without confrontation or serious affront, the presence of minorities and women in the workplace leads to negative action by other members and to the discomfort of members of the majority culture.

Solutions to this problem are discussed in the previous chapter in a section called "Tools for O's." It is advisable for minorities and women workers to study carefully the four stages outlined in Team Building for team membership. Also, minority and women workers will find themselves moving continually among all stages depending upon the content of the perceptions of Caucasian workers on any given day. So, the minority worker may move around from day to day and may be perceived as anything from candidate to finalist to team member to selected member elite.

Adele Scheele's work with careering skills shows that the two groups of workers known as sustainers and achievers are found in different levels as team members. Sustainers could be found waiting for invitations to join teams and might be found in Stages I or II as candidates finalists for team membership. Achievers would be found in States III or IV and would enjoy the privileges and protections of team member or selected team member.

Develop an active sense of humor. Use the humor in situations that could have double meanings. Aim the levity toward reducing the perception of race and sex role stereotyping.

If you continue to be excluded or to be the brunt of negative attention, try to find common goals and interests that are held by you and others and focus on those rather than on differences or the effects of the exclusion.

The second organizational behavior skill is to be able to *exhibit specializing*.

4. Exhibiting specializing means that the individual is being special which leads to recognition and enhancement for the group. This critical career competence is one which allows the worker to prepare by developing and displaying unique talents that are necessary to the group. The skill involved in exhibiting or being special is that the individual captures the attention of the group, makes his talents and abilities available to the group, and uses them to fill the needs of the group.[38]

Belongingness and specializing should both be learned and used as complementary skills. Minorities and women should begin to examine ways of teaching, learning, and sharing, both showing belongingness and exhibiting specialization as complements. Research and biographies about people with successful employment patterns, both male and female, seem to capture a balanced use of both skills.

BUILDING PROFESSIONAL SKILLS

The last set of skills are those used for building professionalism.

5. *Catapulting* involves the two actions of linking the ideas or relationships of one individual with another individual or with a group, and then orbiting into a new world. Catapulting is a new network of connections that would not have been made available without the linking of ideas or relationships with others.[39]

Minorities and women learn this skill for the purpose of linking up with support persons or groups in order to maintain relationships in the world of work that would not otherwise be present. Unlike the team building relationship, catapulting results in the relationship between an individual and a group or person within their same sphere. The advantage of catapulting provides optimum potential for growth because there is movement into another person's world.[40]

The second skill used for building professionalism and for presenting minorities and women in the labor force is the act of *magnifying accomplishments*.

6. Magnifying accomplishments is the act of enlarging, expanding, or broadcasting the group through one's actions. This is a skill that requires obtaining recognition for your work group, organization, or agency from outside persons or organizations.[41] Development of this skill requires the delicate balance of a tightrope walker. If the woman or minority is perceived as a token or a sacrificial affirmative action candidate, the worker is already bringing attention to both self and group. The problem here is that such attention tends to be based on stereotyped views held about minorities and women even in the face of demonstrated competence, talents and abilities. For example, a Black female student made a grade of A on a quantitative chemistry examination at a prestigious university. The Oriental professor gave her a failing grade and wrote on her paper that though he was not sure of how, he was certain that she had cheated on the exam. When questioned, he stated that he was sure that she had cheated because he could not believe that there was a Black woman alive who could make an *A* on his chemistry exam. The student had to seek legal redress to get the grade that she had earned. She went on to work in a large nuclear research laboratory, and was continually bombarded by employment predicaments which stemmed from stereotypes about her race and sex. So, even though her work and qualifications brought notice to the

group, she was seldom able to maneuver that notice for the enhancement of the corporation or herself as an individual.

The Black female scientist began to notice a considerable lessening of adverserial resistance when she married a scientist at the company. She became known as Dr. X's wife. She also sought and gained board membership of a well known civil rights group. That role eased the discomfiture of the Caucasian male scientists as they could understand such roles and involvement. They could accept the magnifying of accomplishments of a Black wife and civil rights activist, but not those of a Black female scientist.

BUILDING COMMUNICATIONS SKILLS

In order to prepare for the world of work, minorities and women must have shaped a system for communications. Everyone must be able to read and to understand what is read. Most important for the minority worker is to read with the understanding that what is written is intended as guidelines, privileges, and procedures for Caucasian males. So, even when what you read clearly indicates that you should have access, you will probably have to apply some pressure to gain access to the bureaucracy.

Timing the application of pressure and an indirect remonstrance may serve as tools. A Black female was asked to provide consulting services to a national organization. She was offered a lucrative contract which required that she perform the services during regular workdays. She applied for vacation time from her regular, salaried job in order to legally receive remuneration for her work. Her boss heard about the dollar amount that she would receive as a consultant and told her that her vacation leave might not be approved. She told him that she would await his decision.

The Black female reviewed the personnel manual and found that she had followed carefully and correctly all procedures. Further, she found no indication that approval of her leave was needed, rather that vacation leave required only prior notification by the employee.

The Black worker carefully chose a Caucasian worker whom she told that she would sue, if denied her right to earned leave. Two days later the supervisor came by to say that he and his boss had decided that this would be a good experience for her to have and so would approve her leave. The Black female replied calmly, "I'm just glad that there is no need for any hassle about this."

Communications skills require that minority workers read, listen, write, and speak with proficiency. While on the job, there is no time or place to relax standard English practices. A high level of English proficiency in reports, memos, letters, and applications is essential to the success of minority workers.

#22   **TOOL FOR SURVIVAL**

When in doubt, check it out. Is the correct spelling professor or proffesor? Is the correct spelling offered or offerred? Should I use "If I were there" or "If I was there"? You need a dictionary, a thesaurus, and a list of 100,000 words at your fingertips at all times. Use them as regularly as your coffee cup.

Whatever you say, hear, and write are a part of a system for presenting yourself in the world of work. The level of proficiency attained represents only one aspect of the impact of presenting yourself using communications skills. Another issue is that different standards apply for minorities and women in the use of communications. These standards differ from those that are expected, anticipated, and accepted for Caucasian workers.

For example, if a Caucasian male supervisor writes a memo to another Caucasian male employee regarding tardiness and/or being away from the job site without standard approval such as a signed travel itinerary, he is judged by co-workers and superiors as "doing his job" or "running a no-nonsense operation." If a minority or woman supervisor wrote the same memo for the same reasons to the same person, she might become the object of the company's investigation. She might be questioned about the nature of the documentation, the amount of counseling done prior to writing the memo, and even whether or not the motivation stemmed from some personality conflict. So the women and minority supervisors must view themselves as a non-traditional entity, who are perceived as having visibility, contrast, and assimilation as special issues related to tokenism. Therefore, women and minority supervisors may need to use non-traditional means to direct the activities of the Caucasian worker.

The adage that "the teacher has to start where the learner is" probably will serve to guide the choices of the women and minority supervisors. When a Caucasian male student, who was a policeman, read *The Autobiography of Malcolm X*, he commented that he "couldn't see why Black people would make such a big deal about identifying with a dope addict and pimp. He was just another example of the ignorant Black man who escaped from reality and was never motivated to better himself." The professor took the student aside and gave him a copy of Bill Russell's *Second Wind*. He looked at the book and said, "Now this is something which I can understand." The professor asked, "Do you know that Russell is married to a Caucasian woman?" The student responded, "Yes, of course, he's just trying to better himself."

Herein lies an example of the perceptions of the Caucasian male that create a Berlin Wall across, and through which flows only the stereotypes that he holds of the Black race. The professor saw the problem being one that is non-traditional in that the job of educating a Caucasian male about race and prejudice became the responsibility of a Black worker.

The problem was further unique in that the student volunteered for the class and sought some new understandings. Lastly, the problem has as a non-traditional thrust, the fact that the student had never discussed his biases in an integrated group using a systematic model for problem solving. Traditional methods such as rap sessions planned to deal with building blocks to understanding for this Caucasian male, could have only added more questions and stirred the flames in an emotional climate. So would the possibility for failure be present for the Black male supervisor if he determined to use traditional forms of reprimand.

Remember that textbook solutions were written for Caucasian males. Management courses are designed for Caucasian males.

Minority and women workers must present themselves as persons who:

1. Generate alternative solutions to problems in the world of work.

2. Develop the courage to risk the use of some alternative plans.

3. Try out different viewpoints and patterns of behavior that may not be obvious to others.

4. Remember that you are a unique worker, your problems are unique and so must your problem solving techniques be unique.

5. Remember that Caucasian workers win-win, win-lose, lose-lose, while minorities and women learn to survive again and again and again.

Unique listening, speaking, reading, and writing skills could provide a positive facet to the communications strategies of minority and women workers. There are some new formations, which when practiced, ease tension and discomfort while bringing about unique and creative solutions to concerns. The paradigm at the bottom of the page gives clues to a positive communications loop for minority and women workers.

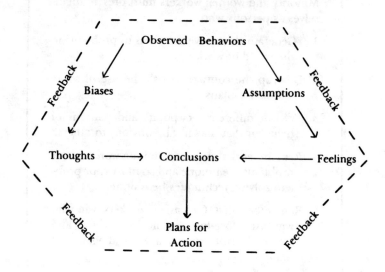

Communications Cycle and Feedback Loop
by: Martha Harris Fair

The communication and feedback loop diagrammed here highlights three important differences, namely:

1. Becoming conscious and aware of and identifying your biases,
2. Taking into account your own feelings as well as the emotional feedback that you gain from others,
3. Planning for action as a dynamic rather than static function.

When tracking down solutions to problems, the communications feedback loop could serve as a tool for the track down. The loop involves minority workers assessing their own beliefs, needs, and value systems. The feedback loop shows that minority women workers must know and understand the lists of things that they hold dear and otherwise value in order to receive uncontaminated information from their personal feedback. The communications feedback loop should then be used for assessment for analyzing and for determining what and where there are needed changes.

Minority and women workers may learn that by finding and admitting their own errors, they might make some constructive adjustments. The loop does not support always looking outside of self for blame or criticism. Rather, use of the communications feedback loop requires minorities and women to see fault in self as well as others. Minorities and women must use tools that do not depend on putting down others or criticizing oneself into an immobilized state. Learning to use these insights allows the worker to move on to more constructive and productive action plans.

EDUCATION AS PREPARATION

The notion that a college education guarantees success is a myth. Formal education, that is the college degree, has been oversold as the panacea that leads directly to job success and job security. Bureau of Census statistics show that from 1980-1990 jobs that require a college education will only comprise 5% of all available jobs while 75% of the jobs available will require technical and/or scientific skills. The other 20% of available jobs will come from the areas of clerical and service industries.

The question is, "What do such statistics mean to workers who wish to develop a positive action plan?" While Caucasian workers may find opportunities for employment when they have the requisite skills or training, minority workers will need both. Through interviews we found minorities in every form of employment working for Caucasians who did not have the same level of college degrees. For example, a Black worker in an academic setting who had earned a doctorate, was told not to put the title Ph.D. on the business card, because such cards brought attention to the fact that the Caucasian chief executive officer did not hold the same credentials.

The positive action plan for Black workers for the 1980's requires that they pursue both the development of marketable skills and the earning of academic degrees. The cost of the terminal degree, Ph.D., is a high cost commodity that rarely reimburses the minority worker in a timely fashion. However, if the worker chooses employment in an academic setting, the Ph.D. is a must for survival.

Betty Lehan Harragan discusses in her book, *Games Mother Never Taught You*, that education has been used as a selecting out process for minorities and women. She documents cases of personnel officers, directors, and chief executive officers who exclude women and minorities from a pool of applicants by stating that, "If you had just completed the next highest degree, we could consider you." Harragan explains the myth of the formal education by showing that these same subjects completed their degrees only to be faced in the next interview with being excluded because they were "over-qualified."

Minorities and women should make a list of seminars, self-help courses, specialized classes, and technical training using time lines as goals for completion. The minority worker must always seek an experience known as a "combo." A combo is both a job that provides gainful employment and formal education through courses, seminars, and training. Social science research shows that women suffer from pay and status reduction whenever they drop out of the labor pool to have children or to increase their skills. Let this serve as a caution to women and minority workers who have considered dropping out of the labor pool to go to school. As a Black activist said during the 1920's: If you're Black, you will have to be ten times as qualified as a Caucasian and still be prepared to have your skills and talents shaded by your skin color.

Minorities and women should consider the purpose of travel to be for both business and pleasure. Self-education has traditionally been an important learning tool for many Black people. Sojourner Truth is portrayed as a woman who could neither read nor write, but there is voluminous evidence of her eloquent and dynamic speeches and debates. Minorities and women should consider accepting volunteer assignments, part-time employment, and other forms of self-education as ways to complement their preparation skills.

NETWORKING AND IMAGE MAKING

Getting along with others is a leadership skill that must be developed in preparation for survival in the workforce. There are four techniques that can be used to develop this second most important skill for employment success. The four techniques outlined below may be used for getting along with others:

1. Create psychic turf through networking,
2. Behave as a professional assertivist by defining your own personal power as a lifetime goal.
3. Conduct your life and relationships at a tempo that could be maintained for the remainder of life,
4. Seek coaching and communications from winners and others with whom you share the same life and employment goals.

Networking is a process by which groups become organized to gain and to give approval, money, access, and protection to members of the group. Carol Kleiman notes that networks, unlike the old consciousness raising groups, do seem to imitate traditional establishment tactics. The key to successful networks should not be to exclude unsuccessful women, but rather to break down barriers for women as a group. [42]

Using carefully directed behaviors and moving from stage to stage, networks can help workers to get along with others. Networking provides a systematic manner in which workers can have their needs and views presented through collective power. Steinem cautions that the behavior of women of all races shows that women "are the only discriminated against group whose members seem to think that, if they don't take themselves seriously, someone else will." [44]

Women and minority workers could learn from other minority groups that techniques for getting along with self and others are a serious endeavor. Joining and participating in networks provides reassurance that you are not an oddball. You can create psychic power and turf as you practice getting along with others in networks.

Networking is a political strategy used to gain professional advantage for the sharing of thoughts, talents, and information. This highly political strategy has but one purpose, which is to mutually benefit the networkers to advance their careers or to expand their power bases in support of their ideas.

When the minority worker enters a new organization, someone will approach and hook them for lunch, which becomes a kind of professional affiliation. The alert and bright minority worker will form no such alliances for the first six months. The key to successful professional affiliations is to remain an autonomous agent who is able to move smoothly among all groups in the organization. Political ties with the right people and conspicuously solid ties with the right people can cause you to be judged in ways that may add to your conflict.

#24   **TOOL FOR SURVIVAL**

People need to know that you care,
Before they care what you know.

or

It is nice to be important, but,
It is more important to be nice.

If successful employment patterns are what you seek, you must work on your skills in dealing with others. Executives admit that when a promotion is in the offing, the first consideration about the candidate is "Can they do the job?" The next is "How does the worker get along with others?"

Networking is done at meetings, receptions, parties, conferences, on-the-job and by phone. When persons ask about networking, the first question is, "Did you leave the proper impression on someone who you hope will do business with you?" Sometimes, the question is, "Did you use the positive image makers, such as the attention lean-in, smile and affirmative nod?'' The positive image makers are required to confirm the art of networking. However, a great deal more is usually happening than is obvious to the active participants. Things happening outside of the immediate network or as a result of the network could be called *"netways."*

Netways differ from traditional networking because of the differences in time factors. The how-tos of networking say that if you attend meetings, gain name-face recognition and become known for the service or product which you represent, business will come to you.

The implication exists that some fairly immediate change will take place. *Netways* might take as long as a year to develop or as little as six to nine months after the initial sharing and connecting of services, resources, ideas, or people takes place. New *netways* could be viewed as micro-miracles in the language of high technology. A micro-miracle takes place when one has no idea that other persons know them, or that others want to connect with them and yet, the linkages and connections happen.

Netways could be great boosters for your business because benefits accrue to you even when you did not purposefully and directly network. *Netways* occur as connections take place over very unusual time periods and distances. The unexpected benefits are the hallmark of *netways*. For example, a speaker benefited from a *netway* when she was recommended by a member of the organization from which she had recently resigned. That *netway* resulted in the delivery of a $500 luncheon address. A large order was phoned in for her book from a party unknown to the author. The caller was the friend of a friend of the consultant who had attended a seminar with the author.

So how do you activate *netways?* You should review what you have done lately. Who have you been serving during the past two years? If you have been actively networking, your phone will start to ring very soon. Happy *NETWAYS!*

TOOL FOR SURVIVAL

Minorities and women are scrutinized closely based on their interpersonal relationships in the workplace. Minorities and women are seldom fired or denied promotion because they fail to do the job tasks or because they lack job skills. Usually Black workers are denied access, influence and promotion because they are considered to have difficulty getting along with and dealing with others.

Networks serve as a good tool. Be skilled at office politics that require that you get along with others at work.

Do not measure success in getting along with others by the social satisfaction of belonging to the clique. Remember cliques can exercise their power by keeping you out or keeping you down.

Minorities and women prepare to survive in the workplace by developing the technique *professional assertiveness*. Professional assertiveness can be contrasted with professional passivism. According to Marilyn Moats Kennedy, career consultant, "The choice all of us face is not whether we're going to get involved; it's where we're going to do it and how."[45] Professional passivity has claimed more victims than monomaniacal bosses and hard job assignments.

Minorities and women have long overestimated the value of hard work, good intentions, and the nose to the grindstone. When careering necessitates the drain of their energies, many employees look the other way. These employees form the vast majority of workers in every organization. However, such workers are not found among those sought after or kept on as new ground is broken and new directions are forged.

Professional assertiveness can be described as the presenting skills that minorities and women use to sell themselves and their achievements. Minorities and women are often uncomfortable when they are expected to brag, to boast of expertise, and to otherwise display their wares. Minorities and women have been observed actually giving credit for their accomplishments to luck. Some minority workers comment that they just happened to be in the right place at the right time. Marilyn Macklowitz calls this phenomenon the "great imposter."[46]

Professional assertiveness means that internal and permanent explanations for success replace external and temporary ones. With all of the mixed messages received in the workplace about only being hired because of affirmative action or about being promoted because of success as a "Tom," Black workers will feel much ambivalence. Such ambivalence encourages the denial of one's own accomplishments and even the sabotaging of one's achievements.

#26   **TOOL FOR SURVIVAL**

Celebrate your accomplishments. Make a concerted effort to build your personal courage for the purpose of accepting your attributes as positive.

Remember any view of yourself that develops because that view is held by others can only be temporary since it only has an external focus. Internalize your view of your strengths. Use your view for professional assertiveness—selling yourself.

Show ownership of your strengths by practicing explaining in action words what you did. Keep track of compliments that you receive.

Minorities and women have at least three options to consider when reviewing a situation involving ways of presenting themselves. The worker may suffer in silence, may shrug off the incident as petty and not accept the affront, or the person may act. Most often any action means some response to the situation. That response could be termed direct confrontation. However, only an extremely naive worker would define professional assertivism as direct confrontation, such as "I want to know if you said what I heard that you said about me."

Professional assertivism skills using direct confrontation for minorities and women should include the following kinds of behaviors:

1. Seek a private time and place.

2. Prepare to fence a bit seeking a draw at the end of the duel which could be called win-win.

3. Avoid accepting the brunt of another person's discontent. You could respond that you prefer an environment that enhances productivity. Also, it is a good idea to indicate that your goal is to act in ways that allow people to work together effectively.

4. Ask for legitimate criticism of your work performance and your attitude.

5. Listen closely to hear breakthrough information even though it may not be totally accurate and may be highly critical. Look for any small grain of truth.

6. Do not retaliate in an irresponsible way.

7. Replace the notions of a friendship fanatic with the understanding that the workplace is a competitive social setting in which those who speak up are the ones who are heard.

8. Prepare to follow your pattern of professional assertiveness for a lifetime.

9. Remember that it does not follow that those who meekly accede to the rules are destined to become victors.[47]

#27   TOOL FOR SURVIVAL

Conduct yourself so that everyday,
in every way
you are an image maker.

Minorities and women should conduct their lives and their

relationships at a tempo that could be maintained throughout a lifetime. Finding one's optimal tempo helps in the presentation of self for two important reasons: (1) First, defining and demonstrating one's tempo consistently is a statement of personal power, and (2) Secondly, any consistently demonstrated maintenance skill can become a weapon against institutional racism and/or sexism and other life changes.

#28   **TOOL FOR SURVIVAL**

Do not start a tempo of work or responses that you cannot maintain over a lifetime.

Accept and demonstrate that the tempo of your work is a phenomenon that effects your introspective thought, abilities, adjustment time, access to resources, ability to identify resources, and your link to the complex affect in organizations.

Remember lions stalk and roam slowly in order to survive in the jungle. Rabbits race about quickly from bush to hole, are eaten, and seldom survive the jungle.

Further preparation that must be accomplished for survival in the workplace includes the worker's attainment of coaching and communications from winners and others with whom they share the same life and employment goals. The similarities among such people would aid in the definition of personal power, and the setting of targets when issues and concerns must be addressed.

The old expression that "no good comes for the preacher talking to the choir because they are all of the same accord," would not apply here. The more minorities and women gain reinforcement for successful patterns and tools for survival, the stronger the worker's level of personal power and coping skills.

#29   **TOOL FOR SURVIVAL**

When "encounters of the third kind" are needed to present yourself in an employment situation, seek coaching and communication with persons who have some knowledge of you and the particular situation. Avoid moan and groan sessions.

Turn up the volume on one of your most powerful communication tools—your listening box.

The "force" is with those who listen to gain an advantage and to those who listen to obtain a victory.

The advantage of the victory spoken of in the tool above refers to both seeking coaching and listening as a communication skill used for the value of gaining access to resources, information, or the job itself. Carol Reed cautioned as she spoke as a household worker and when she resigned from President Carter's National Advisory Committee on Women, "I've never confused access with influence."[48] This statement would serve as a good test for the selection of coaches and communications linkers for minorities and women. "Encounters of the Third Kind" in the workplace require that the minorities and women select coaches who enjoy a bit of both access *and* influence. However, minority workers can probably survive with very little of the so-called free and unsolicited advice. Minorities and women should not sacrifice personal power by habitually accepting unsolicited advice as it tends to have questionable and unsure value.

Dr. Terry Richards says, "It's basic and genetic for the human being to become attached. But we can become attached in a social network."[49] The workplace is a highly complex social network. The workplace requires that we present self and that we sell self in order to survive.

```
┌─────────────────────────────────────────────┐
│                                             │
│  #30      TOOL FOR SURVIVAL                  │
│                                             │
│  Belongingness is a part of your needs system.│
│                                             │
│  The I-can-manage-perfectly-nicely-on-my-own│
│  syndrome characterizes many minority workers│
│  who have fallen as casualities in the workplace.│
│                                             │
│  Do nothing that encourages isolation of yourself on│
│  a job. Seek suitable attachments while defining the│
│  term attachments very loosely.             │
│                                             │
└─────────────────────────────────────────────┘
```

HOW TO PRESENT YOURSELF

This section of the book will provide tools for survival for minorities and women who must present themselves in the world of work. However, along with reporting tools for presenting the self, this section will diagnose and provide prescriptions for the following three areas:

1. Self-assessment for the workplace.
2. Resume writing for employment.
3. Interview skills for careering.

The early 1970's marked an age of what some writers have called "Black capitalism." Implied in the term Black capitalism are notions that support the following assumptions:

1. Black is beautiful even in the workplace.
2. Black people would become established in businesses that were minority-owned firms.
3. Black firms would grow, prosper, and hire Black workers.
4. The bureaucracy would encourage and support Black entreprenuers.
5. The private and the public sectors articulated strong commitments to Blacks as firms, managers, and contractors.[50]

During the 1980's, and most especially as a result of the policies of the Reagan administration, history has begun to repeat itself for minority businesses and minority workers. Historically, minority workers have been underpaid, overworked, treated in careless and callous ways, and have suffered the subtleties of discrimination, ambiguous roles, vague job tasks, and redundant assignments. The serious impact of the non-productive and energy draining phenomena listed point out the advantages to minorities and women who can skillfully and carefully present themselves after self-assessment, through effective resume writing, and with quality interview skills for careering.

Self-assessment for minorities and women depends on the level of development of group and individual identity as reflected in their experiences. Minority group workers' notions about who they are contribute to the development of self-identity and response patterns in the world of work. Definitions and theories abound with regard to the definitions of self-identity. However, Klapp describes it this way:

> "Strictly, it includes all things a person may legitimately and reliably say about himself—his status, his name, his personality, his past life. But if his social context is unreliable, it follows that he cannot say anything legitimately and reliably about himself. His statements of identity have no more reliability than a currency which depends upon the willingness of people to recognize and accept it. We feel that we can count on our identity not only because of habit, but because we can count on people responding to it."[51]

The currency and the self-identity of minorities and women receive recognition and legitimacy from the willingness of others who reserve the right to accept or reject either one. The value of the U. S. dollar responds to the price of gold around the world. So it is with the self-identity of minority workers. Minorities and women struggle for acceptance from others and count on the use of the feedback that they gain for building self-identity.

Racism is the actions, attitudes and institutional structures that subordinate any group of people because of their race. Racism has caused dysfunctional behavior among minorities and women. This dysfunctional behavior has resulted in an unborn self-concept. While many researchers write about low, high, unstable, and disoriented self-concept, our review shows that Blacks can live and die with an unborn self-concept.

The unborn self-concept is the product of the society providing assurance that because of your race or sex you will not be recognized, rewarded, reinforced, stroked, or involved to your full potential. On the other hand, society demonstrates that because of your race and/or sex you must survive, work and live without human connectedness to the majority culture. As minorities and women respond back and forth across these conflicting phenomena, no self-concept is born. The self-concept remains unborn for many until they access their own personal needs system, power, target, and act positively and assertively to give birth to their self-concept.

Minorities and women accept jobs after being told that their titles will be Assistant Vice President or Project Director. They later discover that over golf, cocktails, or in the latrine some new decision has been made. That decision makes them Assistant *to* the Vice President or Consultant at a much lower salary.

In interviews we found two Black workers whose salaries were reduced $3300 and $2500 over a 24 hour period without consultation or reasons provided, and no prior conferences of any kind. We observed one Black male whose salary was frozen, meaning that he did not even receive cost of living or other raises given across the board for four years. Also he was demoted four times in a five year period without a performance evaluation, conference, or consultation. He became lower paid than Caucasian women at the agency with half of his years of seniority. In fact, a Caucasian female who had worked for him at a salary of $16,000 improved her salary by $20,000 within a three year period. She complained about the Black worker as her supervisor and was transferred to another assignment with a $6,000 pay increase. His salary was frozen and he was demoted. She was assigned more responsibility and the next year was paid $29,000. She was awarded a promotion to a job that was never announced by the agency, and she began to supervise programs with budgets well over $10 million. At last review, her salary was listed at $36,000 while the Black male was barely earning $30,000 with fifteen years more seniority. Both parties held terminal Ph.D. degrees.

Such transient career moves cause dysfunctional behavior, cognitive dissonance, and affective disorientation which result in an unborn self-concept.

#31 TOOL FOR SURVIVAL

Self-assessment is a tool which gives birth to the unborn self-concept.

Knowing and confirming one's career and human worth can reduce the adverse effects of job changes such as being denied salary increases and promotions, firing, and layoff.

Knowing how to hit the sweet spot of your racket as one of your I-know-I-can-do-this skills gives you positive direction during employment challenges.

Only the balance between measurement of career worth and human worth for the minorities and women can provide the internal measurement that determines and affirms who you really are.

The labor pains of self-assessment are worth it, as they assure the birth of the *unborn self-concept* in the form of a healthy entity.

The importance of self-assessment as a tool for survival cannot be overemphasized. Self-assessment means that you ask yourself questions such as:

1. What do I like?
2. What do I dislike?
3. Which things create irreconcilable differences for me?
4. What am I sure that I know?
5. How do I feel when I hit the "sweet spot in my racket?"

Analyses of the responses to these questions represent the labor pains. The answers to these questions represent the birth of the unborn self-concept. Such introspection and the resulting responses significantly lower the level of adverse influence from outside. Contamination readings are significantly reduced by the flow of the internal power source from information and feedback produced by self-assessment.

Self-assessment should be done using questions from the two categories: (1) self-assessment of human worth, and (2) self-assessment of career worth. I have chosen these two categories because of the dichotomy that is maintained as they are both operationalized. The two categories function as clear choices to be made when minorities and women look for work. These questions should be added to those that ask about prestige, important title, and salary. Self-assessment is the goal of responses to the following lists of questions:

Career Worth	Human Worth
1. How am I valued on my job?	1. What value do I place on knowing other people?
2. What is the short term value of my job?	2. What value do I place on gaining new knowledge?
3. What is the long term worth of my career choice?	3. What is the worth of my conflict resolution skills?
4. Is my career worth the strain that I feel because of its many demands?	4. What is the value to me of being confident about my strengths and competencies?
5. What is the value of the support that I receive on my job?	5. What is the value of the support that I provide for my peers, family, parents, and friends?

Career counseling has grown in importance because the answers to questions about career and human worth may not be easily ascertained. Some workers have used Performax materials and the Myer Briggs Inventory to systematize their responses for purposes of self-assessment.

The most important thing to note about examining career worth-human worth is that self-assessment of one's human worth comes primarily from self. Self-assessment asks for answers derived internally, and heavily relies on the development of personal goals, individual objectives, and the recognition of personal power. The opposites are often true of the assessment of career worth alone. Career worth responses require external reports, the bestowing of power from others, the confirmation of titles from others, and the transient protection of members of a group.

Minorities and women must assess both their human and career worth and clearly know the value of each as they perceive them. When job changes occur—firing, demotion, salary freezes, discriminatory practices, and other adversities—the balance created by self-assessment from both categories will sharply reduce the effects on the ability to survive. The fact may be that you've been fired or have not won a promotion. But the truth is that because you are a worthy human being *all things work together for good*, even when others mean them to harm you.

The Career Quest Test by Kate Vozoff has been added here as an instrument to be used by minorities and women for self-assessment. You should be able to discern some of your career strengths and weaknesses. You should be able to find areas in which you are struggling with decision-making. Your answers should show you other areas where you find yourself misinterpreting or confused about the use of politics and personal power.

C. Q. Test: Career Quest Test

1. Organizations require workers to engage in political games which:

   a. are a destructive waste of time.
   b. concern everyone who wants to get ahead.
   c. are exciting because they bring you into contact with people.

2. When I am isolated from the office team, I:

   a. work harder at specific job tasks, and ignore the alienation.
   b. try repeatedly to show people that I am not as different as I seem.
   c. keep my hurt feelings to myself.

3. The company gossips are:

   a. angry people whose attitudes have nothing to do with me.
   b. resentful of me although they are not able to tell me why.
   c. people who should be replaced by more professional employees.

4. Though my work is well done and on time, my boss appears disappointed with me. I guess that the boss:

   a. will eventually get over it.
   b. defines good work differently than I do, and it is the boss's opinion that counts.
   c. is threatened by my potential.

5. When a co-worker spreads gossip about me, I:

   a. ignore it and seek support of family and friends.
   b. look for a private moment to ask what is disturbing about my work or attitude.
   c. ask my supervisor for confidential advice.

6. My rule for maintaining a good network of associates is to:

   a. minimize the appearance of obvious ambitions by associating with people outside the company.
   b. occasionally socialize with co-workers that I most admire.
   c. spend time really getting to know the people with whom I work each day.

7. The successful professional:

   a. keeps personal relationships out of the office.
   b. works as a member of the team but calls it quits at closing time.
   c. fosters and nurtures friendships with co-workers as they are the people with whom you have the most in common.

8. The best plan for beginning a new job is:

   a. to focus attention on the work and stay out of trouble.
   b. give yourself six months and then assert yourself for the purpose of advancement.
   c. coalesce and gain support early as a way to cope with organizational politics.

9. Cliques in an organization are:

   a. trouble, trouble, double-trouble.
   b. tempting, but dangerous because we're judged by the company we keep.
   c. one way to personalize an otherwise cold, impersonal, and bureaucratic environment.

10. Getting along well at work is:

    a. not nearly as important as getting the job done.
    b. harder to do than I used to think.
    c. easy for well-adjusted individuals.

11. In order to get along with my associates, I:

    a. refuse to be distracted by those who are relentlessly obnoxious.
    b. intend to go more than halfway as long as I am getting ahead.
    c. have the right to expect them to try to get along with me.

12. My pattern for job success is:

    a. to work hard, be honest, and you'll get the professional recognition that you deserve.
    b. to master the art of career politics and practice it at all times.
    c. to be the warmest person that I can and to know that my co-workers will not only admire me but will like me as well.

Adapted from Equal Opportunity Forum—by Kate Vozoff.

Career Quest Test Answers Below

eyes and quietly do the job but only assertive involvement will place you at the top.

On the other hand, if you tended to answer "b" more times than not, you're destined for either change or a chronic case of wounded feelings. Work will never satisfy all your personal needs, so re-think your on-the-job expectations.

There may be those who in all sincerity whizzed through the questions circling "c" (for balance) as they went. If you're one of them, congratulations. You are the perfect combination, acknowledging the realities of power play yet clear on the distinction between professional commitment and personal need. Better hold on to your hat. You're not just moving toward success—you're in orbit.

Can you count yourself among the surprisingly small group of up-and-comers who juggle power in just the right way? In the spirit of true exchange, this quiz and article have been designed not to create or nurture competition but to help you pinpoint career strengths and weaknesses. On this very evolved note, let us dispense with grades and speak instead of tendencies.

If deep down, you found yourself most often attracted to "a" answers, then you are one of the many who tussle with professional passivity. It may be easier to pull the blanket of dedication over your

Minorities and women as workers must be carefully marketed. Careful marketing has as a first requirement that you pinpoint potential prospects who might buy you, the product. There are four tools used to market minority workers. They are: (1) the letter of application, sometimes called the testimonial letter, (2) the resume, (3) the interview, and (4) negotiations.

LETTER OF APPLICATION

The letter of application, which is sometimes called the testimonial letter, should follow these guidelines:

1. No more than 1½ to 2 pages.
2. Typed with no errors. Proofread carefully. Watch spelling and sentence structure.
3. Try to use descriptive language that shows how you increased profits to your agency.
4. Avoid self-evaluation, just state facts.
5. Avoid abbreviations and "refer to resume."
6. Present your qualifications honestly.
7. Let your measured accomplishments make the strength of your letter.
8. Tailor your letter for each application to show how you have bonafide occupational qualifications.
9. Use the language of the job description and describe your skills as they relate to the job criteria.
10. Your letter of application or testimonial letter is separate from your application form and your resume.

Your letter of application or testimonial letter should include the following:

1. A statement about the job for which you are applying. Example: I am writing this letter to apply for the position of . . . .
2. A statement about why you are interested in the position. Example: As principal of the school for the gifted, I developed, planned, and implemented curriculum innovations in science, math, and reading.
3. Statements (3–5) about your strengths and special qualifications for the job. Example: A few of my other accomplishments are: Reduced labor cost by 10 percent and increased productivity by differentiated staffing programs that I developed.
   NOTE: Be sure to place your measured achievements at the beginning of each statement for heaviest impact.
4. Closing statement including your wish to discuss further details in an interview.

THE RESUME

The resume is a presentation tool that is often overlooked and unbelievably shabbily prepared by some workers. However, this may be your only chance to look different from your competition in order to get the interview that you need to complete the marketing of yourself. Your resume functions as your second sales tool. Your first selling tool is you. Remember, no one and nothing can sell you as well as you sell you.

Resumes should be written to assure a potential employer that you would be a good investment for their company. The person reading your resume must feel that you are a profit-producer, that you understand the world of business, and that you will remain profit-conscious in the future. Use descriptive phrases that document, measure, and quantify your achievements.

Here is a checklist of Do's and Don'ts to consider as you prepare your resume:

1. *Do not* write vague, puffy, subjective sentences.
2. *Do* include all skills that you have that would contribute to the profit-making side of the agency or organization.
3. *Do not* decide that your area of specialization cannot be quantified and therefore cannot be thought of as profit-

producing. Find opportunities to express your job tasks as increases and profit-makers.

4. Remember to write about the product, you, from the point of view of what it can do for the buyer, the potential employer.
5. Use short sentences and short words when they provide the meaning intended.
6. Be sure to take credit for work done under your direction. Emphasize your achievements.
7. *Do not* boast, but be honest if you had certain responsibilities.
8. Be sure to take with you from each job copies of documentation of commendations that you keep in your home file.
9. *Do not* write a resume that is an attendance record. Try to communicate and to persuade.
10. *Do not* use glowing generalities. Be specific.[52]

Resumes must be written, but great restraint should be used before sending one out. Note the example of a minority worker who left work in the public sector to work in the private sector. He only sent out his resume after he was assured of personal interviews. He learned that whenever he sent his resume to companies who promised interviews after receipt of the resume, he received "Dear John" letters that stated "after careful review of your qualifications, no thanks." He observed that sending the resume with no personal contact or appointment for an interview was a sure loser. The clerk (called an "application flow specialist") decided that she didn't like the "hype" or he wasn't her type. The employer who hired him did not ask for a resume.

INTERVIEWS

Interviews can be generated by use of direct mail, personal or phone contacts. Your testimonial letter mailed to the president of a company can spell out your achievements and result in being selected for an interview. The same testimonial letter sent to the personnel department gets a "Dear John" response. A letter to the president causes some action. Presidents, managers, and supervisors can pass instructions down the line to subordinates with instructions to do something for this person.

Black workers need as much reach as possible to market themselves. *Reach* is a marketing term that means that a commercial message has been sent through the maze and has arrived at the point where corporate decision-making takes place. Personnel departments are deadly for minorities and women because personnel specialists are eager to build a volume of paperwork and to maintain massive files. They justify their existence by developing new forms and new applications. The most important caution to minorities and women is that we represent an important statistic to personnel departments: it is called "minority applicant flow." An invitation to apply for a job may be legitimate or it may be a strategy designed to show minority applicant flow. However, after rejection of the minority applicant, the personnel division may design a rating form which shows that certain people were rejected because:

1. They were overqualified.
2. Their application packet was incomplete.
3. Their salary level had been higher, so they wouldn't have been happy here.
4. They seemed emotionally ill-equipped for work on a sophisticated team.

If you receive an invitation for an interview, you are probably perceived as a well-organized achiever who could be a success. You should prepare for the interview as if you expect to go to work the next day. There is no way to get a job without a face-to-face encounter.

You may be interviewed by any number of people from one to twenty. It is necessary that you try to win each one. The best impression for minorities and women to leave is that you would be a "nice person" to have around the agency, organization, or corporation. To prepare for the interview:

1. Do homework on the company in order to know as much about it as possible.
2. Review the job announcement. Extrapolate the job expectations. Careful here; make inquiries when you are not certain.
3. Prepare a three-minute verbal presentation as the response to the question, "Will you tell us about yourself?"
4. Rehearse your response to "Why have you applied for this job?"
5. Rehearse your answers out loud using complete sentences.
6. Rehearse telling about three of your strengths that relate directly to the job expectations.

7. Prepare a response to show how you turn a weakness into a strength.

#32   **TOOL FOR SURVIVAL**

Never say "No, I don't know anything about
_____ " or "No, I've never done any _____ ."
You could say "My experience with _____
prepared me to do _____ ." Or "I did not have
total responsibility for _____ but I worked with
_____ directly," or "I was aware of its operation
because of my task in the area of _____ ."[53]

Know that communication includes agreements to send and to receive messages. You will be sending messages during the entire time on-site as well as during the formal interview. Remember to:

1. Give a cheerful greeting. Speak to everyone.
   Take time to nod, acknowledge and position your chair in order to ease down.

2. Smile and appear comfortable.
   Smile and concentrate on your breathing for four seconds. In, two-three-four, out, two-three-four and repeat.

3. Sit relaxed with good posture.
   Find comfortable places and ougles for your hands. Resist knuckle cracking, handwringing, and finger pyramiding.

4. Demonstrate a sense of humor.

    Look for an acceptable point for levity. Be careful that you do not attempt humor at some's expense.

5. Answer questions succinctly and precisely.

    Some questions can be appropriately answered with yes or no. When longer responses are needed, answer only the questions that you are asked. Do not oversell. Organize your response before you speak.

6. Summarize only long answers.

    Your summary should bring the point of your conversation into clear focus. You may not have another chance to divulge your meaning.

#33   **TOOL FOR SURVIVAL**

Listen. Listen. Listen as if your life depends on receiving good quality information.

Demonstrate a willingness to learn and to work.

Demonstrate your expertise and knowledge.[54]

According to Sylvia Porter, 99-100 percent of all American companies use the interview as a selection tool for hiring decisions. Polishing your interview skills is an essential for survival in the world of work. You have prepared by rehearsing your responses; now you must sharpen your interview technique.

Know the size, income, image, problems, competition, history, and philosophy of the company.

Respond concisely to questions. Before you resort to over-elaboration, ask the interviewer if more details are necessary.

If you do not understand a question, ask for clarification before you attempt a chance answer.

Respond to the question. Do not volunteer information unless it is relevant and positive.

Save your big hits for later when the interviewer has gained momentum.

Strive for a natural dialogue. But allow the interviewer to set the pace and to control the conversation.

Turn up your antennae for signals that you need to read about the interviewer. The *interviewer* may be nervous if this is his first interview.

Be prepared for the basic seven:
(1) Tell me about yourself.
(2) What can you offer us?
(3) What are your strengths?
(4) What have you accomplished?
(5) What are your limitations?
(6) How much are you worth?
(7) What is your salary need?

Prepare a few questions for the interviewer.[55]

If you decide that you are seriously interested and the interviewer seems to be ready to hire you, prepare for negotiations. Negotiations are a different method for presenting yourself to an employer. The Black worker will find that negotiating skills need a great deal of practice, and will find the skills need to be different as they move to different fields. According to Dr. Barbara Swaby, a professor at the University of Colorado at Colorado Springs, Black workers must practice negotiations because:

> ". . . the passive aggressive, subtle negativism is so entrenched in the culture that the effects constantly affect one's professional existence."[56]

Swaby further states that:

> ". . . Blacks gear all professional activities at weakening the chain of negativism . . . striving toward financial independence . . . in order to achieve economic freedom through developing financial expertise. . . ."[57]

Financial expertise requires that Black workers build negotiating skills. Financial expertise for Black workers means lifting one's worth out of the bargain basement mentality. The negotiations conversation should begin by your naming a figure that is higher than you expect to get. Saltovstall says to name a figure that is 20 percent more than you expect to get. Black workers should perhaps use only 10 percent higher as realistic because they will be quizzed about justification of their worth based on perceptions that will never be verbalized. Blue-collar work scales are so set that no reduction in opening figures should be necessary. The reality is that no matter what the Caucasian employer's verbal response is, what is meant would be, "We don't pay our Caucasian males that much; why should we consider this for a Black."

The employer's response will probably go something like this, depending on how badly he wants you: "We've never started anyone that high." You respond that the company has no one with your skills. The employer will counter offer, and you say, "I hope we can agree on a satisfactory figure." If the employer lowballs you, then ask if he can make an offer somewhere in the middle of the range.

Negotiating Steps

Some steps that should take place when negotiating are:

1. Name a salary that is higher than you expect to get in order to give yourself room to negotiate.
2. Don't rush. Let the boss respond. Go step by step.
3. Plan a few minor concessions—things that you can live without. Give them away one at a time.
4. Don't be afraid of silence. Write the counteroffer on a pad and just sit quietly. Count to 20.
5. Do not repeat the employer's statement. Go on to your need. For instance, you might say, "I had in mind a combination with a final package of a salary of $25,000." Then be quiet.
6. If asked how you arrived at your figure, say, "This is what is paid in our area right now. I checked with companies X and Y."
7. Take each issue point by point. Talk salary, then vacation, then pension, then expense account. Only use these as linkages if you reach an impasse.
8. Remember, you do not have to beat the boss; you are merely trying to reach a mutual agreement that is a good bargain for both of you. You should each be engaged in a win-win negotiation which allows both of you to get what you want.[58]

Some employers use the take-it-or-leave-it announcement early in negotiations. The worst thing to do is to assume that you've lost and this is the end. Use silence to re-focus on your goals and to cast away negative emotions. Then try three tactics, such as:

1. "I think you'd agree that $_____ does not apply to my experience over a period of _____ years with a broad base of responsibility," or
2. "You would benefit from my ability to do _____ for your company, which would earn an added _____ percent of income. Therefore, your offer does not reflect my value to you," or
3. "Your offer is very low, but I might accept it if my salary is raised to my expectation after three months, in which I would have had time to demonstrate my abilities."[59]

You have reacted positively, you have discouraged the ultimatum, and you have suggested positive negotiating results.

#35   TOOL FOR SURVIVAL

1. Avoid snap decisions. Ask for time to think over the offer.
2. Set goals and targets. What do you want and what will you ask?
3. Do not be awed by experts. Do not devalue your skills.
4. Be prepared to negotiate. Find some things that you can live without.
5. Have some knowledge of other potential employers' motives.
6. Stay unemotional, cool, and objective. Do not appear aloof or apathetic.
7. Try to have consistency in your tone of voice, body movements, and facial expressions.
8. Be assertive, not aggressive, enough to get what you want.
9. Have a win-win attitude. Remember even *no* can change from *maybe* to *yes*.
10. If negotiations falter, tactfully ask for a recess. Be specific about a time to reconvene. You may need time to reinforce your confidence, compose yourself, rebuild your positive thoughts, and review both your opponent's and your own positions.[60]

The negotiations process assumes the same agreements as the communications process. In both instances two parties must agree to discuss one topic, and that they want to work toward resolutions. There have been instances in which I found that I worked for an organization which considered negotiations as strictly a process used by Caucasians only. Just as in schools sometimes grades of "C" stand for colored, so it is in some agencies, organizations, and corporations that the lowest salaries stand for all colored peoples.

For example, a minority female compiled a packet of materials for a negotiating session. Then, she asked her boss if they could discuss her salary. He agreed. After she named her price, he said, "Miss X, you are a credit to your race. You are one of the most powerful Black women in our state. So you have already been compensated for your outstanding work. Besides that, you don't really need more money." She smiled and asked if he really thought her professional goal was to become a credit to her race. He smiled back and said, "Facts are facts." She asked him if he could provide her with something to spend in the grocery store. He replied that her diamond pendant indicated she was doing okay. She asked whether he was aware that all Caucasians in the agency with her level of responsibility were paid at higher levels than she, and that they did not hold terminal degrees. He said, "Yes, but your husband makes a good living on his job."

The minority female asked for a recess. She began to look for other work, did not find suitable employment, and, one year later, resigned. There have been complaints brought and won by three other minority employees in that agency since she left. Her only real struggle was to determine whether or not to use her energies filing and winning a discrimination suit, or moving on to new ventures. She chose the latter.

Even in retrospect, she is happy that she gave the agency no more of her time or energy. The permanence of racism and sexism were so deeply embedded that even protest required more than good will and an education about discrimination, and far more than she was willing to invest. Besides that, the payoff would have been to remain there with the onslaught of ethnic jokes, bigoted remarks, biased policies, and blatantly prejudiced behaviors. Moving out of and away from an agency must be one of the positive options when negotiations are not considered a legitimate strategy for women and minority workers.

It is more important for minorities and women to know what they think of the organization than to know what the agency, institution, or organization thinks of them before starting a new job.

Information is power. The best alliances are formed with persons with whom you can share information. Minority and women workers should be cautious about sharing their personal views and opinions about the job and the people.

Fernandez points out that power and politics are reflected by the feelings, attitudes, and actions of Blacks and can be understood by looking at the lifestyle profiles of some Black workers in predominantly Caucasian organizations. He notes four distinctly different styles that gain specific and different responses from each group. Fernandez states that the characteristics are seen in a range of behaviors from assimilative to non-assimilative.

BLACK MALE—29 years old:

1. Works at bank in Black community.
2. Boyhood spent in Missouri.
3. Went to college at Golden Gate College.
4. Married and lives in 70% Black neighborhood.
5. Democrat.
6. Baptist, but does not go to church.
7. Active in the NAACP, the Urban League, ACLU, and has Caucasian friends.
9. *Philosophy:*
   a. Work in parallel systems to establish strong Black social, political, and economic organizations.
   b. Marriage to a Caucasian could be okay.
   c. Doesn't get along with militants, but feels that you must pressure Caucasians for Black equality.
   d. It is only the militants who call him an Uncle Tom.
   e. Believes that society has not changed and would not accept a transfer to a small, predominantly Caucasian city.
   f. Believes in social change as we keep our traditions and characteristics and gain acceptance on our own terms.

Conclusion: Fairly assimilative attitudes and behaviors.[62]

BLACK MALE—28 years old:

1. In corporation for 2½ years.
2. Born and raised in California. Went to school for finance degree at Berkeley.
3. Married and lives in San Francisco.
4. Lives in 95% Black community.
5. No religious preferences. Attends church a few times a year.
6. Democrat.

7. Belongs to no organizations and has little contact with whites.
8. Would not consider marriage to a Caucasian.
9. *Philosophy:*
   a. Has no common ground with Caucasians except that he has to work with them.
   b. Has friends from all segments.
   c. Feels that Blacks can only gain experience from Caucasian corporate world.
   d. Racial bigotry is permanent.
   e. A new nation for Blacks our only option.

Conclusion: Extremely non-assimilative.[63]

BLACK FEMALE—41 years old:

1. Began work as a stenographer.
2. Worked up to lower management after 13½ years.
3. From Texas.
4. Baptist and attends church twice monthly.
5. Democrat.
6. Belongs to NAACP and all-Black social clubs.
7. Outside of work, little contact with Caucasians.
8. Has never been called a "sellout" or an "Uncle Tom."
9. *Philosophy:*
   a. Does not like militants because of their violent tactics.
   b. Would not transfer to a small Caucasian town because she'd not be accepted.
   c. Blacks must make Caucasians aware of the need for changes in housing, jobs, and finance.
   d. Blacks do not want to assimilate, but want to be able to live free and equal lives.

Conclusion: Quite non-assimilative.[64]

BLACK FEMALE—49 years old:

1. Lived in Utah and California.
2. Father civil service supervisor.
3. Married, lives in all-Caucasian neighborbood in San Francisco.
4. Methodist and attends church a few times a year.
5. Democrat.

6. Belongs to several business and civic groups with Caucasian members.
7. Has frequent contacts with Caucasians at parties and social functions.
8. Could easily marry a Caucasian.
9. *Philosophy:*
   a. Blacks must function in any community. Would move to another all-Caucasian town if needed.
   b. Believes that Caucasian business world does not interfere with Blacks' allegiances to their own community.
   c. Best path for Blacks is total integration and complete assimilation with Caucasians. Nothing else will work.

Conclusion: Extremely assimilative.[65]

As these four sets of attitudes, feelings, and philosophies indicate, views among Blacks differ about their own actions in the world of work. Each Black sees the source and use of power in a different way. While swimming with sharks in the world of work, the Black worker should consider that there are changing central views about the provision of equal employment opportunities for Blacks by both Blacks and Caucasians.

Robert Blauner has suggested that some of these changing views exist because of the new phenomenon of today called neoracism. Blauner points out that:

"It is still difficult for most whites to accept the unpleasant fact that America still remains a racist society. Such an awareness is further obscured by the fact that the more sophisticated, subtle, and indirect forms, which might better be termed, neoracism, tend to replace the traditional, open forms that were most highly elaborated in the old South."[66]

#38 **TOOL FOR SURVIVAL**

Minorities and women must now cope with neo-racism—the covert, subtle, sophisticated, and complex racial discrimination that excludes them from participation in the world of work.

Neoracism is demonstrated in the exclusions of minorities and women based on objections such as:

1. You are overqualified.

2. Your style of dress and personal mannerisms offend other co-workers in the organization.

3. You would not be happy at the upper level because Caucasians are not ready to accept you.

4. You do not have the proper qualifications for Board level membership.

5. You were not the "best" qualified candidate for upper-level managerial positions.

6. You would perform better in jobs directly connected to the minority consumer market or other minority personnel.

A Black female experienced the insidiousness of neoracism when she was removed as a project director from an advocacy program for race and sex equity by the chief executive officer. He reassured her that she was not being fired, because she had done extraordinary work for three years. He went on to indicate that he was reassigning her to some other program because programs dealing with concerns for minorities were "not good for her." She asked what had made him decide these things and in what new area had he decided that she could serve better. He replied, "Oh, I don't really want to go into any specifics. I'll think of something in a couple of days and let you know what I've decided. You can just come to work and let your Caucasian secretary take messages for a couple of days while I decide."

The Black female asked if something had happened to cause this decision. The chief executive officer indicated that he had heard that the organization's printer had missed a deadline and that there had been harsh words between the project director and the printer. The project officer responded that 100 training manuals, ordered six months before the seminar date, had not been delivered as promised. She had talked to the printer about the importance of meeting promised deadlines. She asked what was improper or objectionable about such an exchange. The chief executive officer offered, "Oh, that doesn't matter really, I've just decided to reassign you when I've decided what to do with you." The project director spent the weekend trying to find out what the catalyst had been for such a decision. She found that her Black male supervisor had asked for her dismissal because they did not share the same management style.

The Black female decided to resign immediately. However, she asked for six months' salary to be paid while she sought another position. She received six months' pay, but never a letter responding in any way to her resignation. Six months later, the Black male supervisor was fired with six months' pay to find another job.

In the preceding example, neoracism, sexism, and institutional racism and sexism are all at work together. Institutional racism is at work, as delineated by Baron, when:

> "The individual generally does not have to exercise a choice to operate in a racist manner. The rules and procedures of the large organizations have already prestructured the choice. The individual only has to conform to the operating norms of the organization and the institution will do the discriminating for them."[67]

Here the attitudes of Caucasians are not important. The institutional structures are actually used to exclude minorities and women. On the positive side, you may not change attitudes, but you can change structures.

Minorities and women face the self-perpetuating characteristics of institutional racism.

Government regulations and affirmative action programs have checked the deleterious effect of institutional racism on minority workers. The sad fact is that both regulations and programs have been weakened by the Reagan administrative policies.

Hiawatha Roosevelt Harris, late father of the author, once said "Blacks must be eternally vigilant in their fight for equal opportunity. The over-comers will be counted among those who fought on and on and on."

James Reynolds, retired Director of the Civil Rights Commission in Denver, said, "The victors will not be rabbits who are swift, but will be lions who are strong and determined to survive in the jungle filled with predators."

Minorities and women may "give in" from the sheer fatigue of the constant injustices imposed upon them, but they must *never* "give up."

Frederick Douglass reinforced these beliefs when he wrote in 1849 that:

"The limits of tyrants are prescribed by the endurance of those whom they suppress."[68]

A group of Caucasian workers mentioned that the upwardly mobile, super-educated, talented, and sought-after Black worker has now become a dinosaur. The Caucasians indicated that Black workers are growing extinct, becoming fossilized, and will be studied in the future as an anomaly. Herein, we find an example of hardening racist attitudes that have found a comfortable climate of support in the moral majority, in right-wing politics, and in

Caucasian male-dominated organizations.

We find that Caucasians openly express more anger, defensiveness, and hostility as we observe the covert activities of the Ku Klux Klan. By contrast, Blacks have become more impatient, more demanding, and more militant as evidenced by the recent activities of Reverend Jesse Jackson's threat to boycott Coca-Cola, and his 1984 candidacy for President.

"When" and "what" will minority workers overcome is no longer a viable question to ask. In the words of Hiawatha Roosevelt Harris, well-known community leader, dynamic speaker, and educator, the final outcomes are delayed because,

> "If the American white man has not prepared enough Black workers to work beside him, his institutions have failed both the Black and the Caucasian races."[69]

This book was written with the hope that as minorities and women swim with sharks, they will develop new skills using their tools for survival. Further, it is believed that there may be found in this book some tools for harmonious life and growth for all of the persons in the world of work.

Swimming With Sharks

CHAPTER FOUR

CHAPTER FOUR

"You may have intelligence and ability, but you still need will power and drive to succeed."

— Fred Brum

Swimming With Sharks

The illustration chosen for this chapter was used to test the responses of the minorities and women in the 1980's to their feelings about the world of work. Whether minorities and women were found in agencies, public or private sector, or corporations, their responses, without exception, were, "This is just how I feel every day," or "That is how I survive. I swim with sharks," and "Those who don't survive are eaten by the sharks. Some poor swimmers are just killed by the sharks for sport." This chapter is written to formulate tools for survival for all swimmers. These tools are produced to help poor swimmers to improve their skills, and to establish minorities and women as survivors who maintain economic independence and financial stability.

Both before the job and after gaining the job, minorities and women face the issues of geography and property rights. Successfully swimming with sharks means that minority workers demonstrate an awareness of their sense of belongingness as correlated with where my people are, where I first dug my fingers into the soil, or where I spent summers with my grandparents. Geography is then a part of the sense of where Black workers belong.

"Away from one's home and people, one is merely a sojourner. . . . Cleveland may represent merely a forty-seven year visit away from home. Thus our brother is never in a true sense a Clevelander. However much his community makes him feel an outsider, he himself provides an additional increment of alienation. As a protective device, he says it was never his city anyway."[70]

Protective devices are often used by minorities and women in the employment arena to reduce the shock of the subtle alienation and attacks on the job. Such attacks threaten the property rights and employment opportunities of minority workers. Traditionally, America's Black workers have worked with Caucasians and lived with other Blacks. Black workers made a living environment for themselves by attempting assimilation, by supporting integration, or by withholding themselves from any relationships with others that were not work related. Some Black workers use other tactics in order to rebel against the alienation and oppression in the environment. One example of such a technique of rebellion is tardiness. Being tardy is a statement that says, "I will not pretend that I am important. So I withhold my presence."

Affirmative action programs of the 70's tended to reduce the need for such behaviors for two reasons:

1. Minorities and women sought legal redress as it was unlawful for the blatant discriminatory practices to be used against them in employment.
2. More minorities and women were hired, reducing tokenism in organizations, agencies, and institutions.

A healthy economy and government pressure pushed along together and added to the minority worker's way stations in the world of work. According to Amal Nag, staff reporter for *The Wall Street Journal* in the 1980's, minorities and women are losing the employment gains of the 70's as the economic boom evaporates.[71]

The questions then become, Do minorities and women move from victors to victims, and What can be done and how much can be done to assure that these workers survive?—that is, find new ways to swim with sharks in the world of work. Changes in economic policies, and business and industrial output, will affect all workers. To some degree then, all workers will become victims as they seek change. However, there is no need for, nor any time for, defeatist attitudes for minorities and women who seek to survive through use of skills with successful employment patterns as outcomes.

The family of Black folk is broad. The self has its roots in many places. Brothers and sisters have their work selves and their personal selves. The Black worker as a creature of prey must have more than one haven.

"It's a poor rat that don't have but one hole."[72]

Work Caucasian, live Black with home as your sanctuary. Invite into your home loved ones, trusted friends and soulmates.

Politics, receptions, and obligatory social functions belong at the Holiday Inn.

Victors share the many characteristics derived from triumph, success, winning, mastery, and awards of prizes. The two categories that must be examined by minorities and women who become victors are:

1. Techniques and tactics for guerrilla warfare; and
2. Techniques for career empowerment (how to get what you want and need from your job and how to maximize your level of satisfaction).

Guerrilla warfare is defined as the harassing of a large army by small units or bands engaging in quick, carefully targeted combat. The large body is hit with frequent, small, and powerful blows that eventually weaken the legs and bring down the head to a vulnerable level.

Some advantages of guerrilla warfare for women and minority workers in the labor force are:

1. You do not need large numbers of people to mobilize and to have impact;
2. You can concentrate on one cause or target at a time;
3. The enemy is never sure of how much you know, where you will strike next time, or which tools you will use; and
4. Guerrilla warfare is conducive to states of creative tension for both ally and foe.

#41   **TOOL FOR SURVIVAL**

Guerrillas in the jungle survive because of the carefully planned tactics that assure small victories.

Guerrilla warfare is guided by the philosophy of use of the "threat of" rather than "threatening to." The "threat of" any number of things that could happen is far more powerful than the announcement of a single threat.

The disadvantages of guerrilla warfare are as follows:

1. Though only small units or bands of people are needed, they must make a long term commitment in order to serve effectively;
2. You must be prepared to accept some lose-lose, win-lose, and/or some win-win results;
3. If the chief executive officer changes your responsibilities, then you must change your targets and objectives;
4. You must be certain of who your adversaries are and what their motives are;

5. Test your strategies to determine whether or not you have weakened your adversary. If you received inaccurate information and find yourself attacking in an area where the adversary is strong and fortified, a hasty retreat should be ordered.

#42   **TOOL FOR SURVIVAL**

Agree with thine adversary quickly.

Do not lament — DOCUMENT.

Practice stalking like a lion, team building like a herd, striking like a leopard. Use concrete issues as weapons, and whenever you must, retreat gracefully without fanfare.

Women and minority workers who are victors must use all of their strokes as they swim with sharks. Because the breast stroke uses the coordination and combination of all other strokes, it represents knowledge of all of the rules and regulations of the organization. The side stroke represents the efforts of minorities and women toward filtering the published rules and regulations in order to determine how that worker must function within the organization. The backstroke represents the contemplative stroke used when women and minority workers must examine the possible pitfalls from such activity as receiving damaging memoranda, the political cost of having expressed opinions on issues that arise, or the invisible jeopardy in putting issues, concerns, orders, and directives into writing.

Minorities and women must read, know, and understand the formal rules and regulations that govern their organizations.

Minorities and women must gain information about the formal enabling legislation or company policy that was used to establish their division, unit, or program.

Though the organization may actually break all of its own rules and regulations, minorities and women must know the content of the legislation, personnel handbooks, fiscal management procedures, and other guidelines. Every private corporation has bylaws set by a board of directors. The private sector has other guidelines that establish how the industry, company, or business will be operated. Every public organization was formed by and is operated by laws passed.

#43　　　　**TOOL FOR SURVIVAL**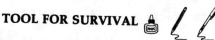

Know the rules and regulations that govern the organization.

Know what the book says about the goals, objectives, powers, and duties for each segment of the organization.

Your survival may depend on the fact that you know what the policy says while the organization breaks its own rules every day. When you face a trouble spot, you may be able to save yourself using the fact that the agency has broken its own written policies and regulations.

Operationalize Your Personal Action Plan

Knowledge of standard operating procedures would help you to understand your job responsibilities and what you can and cannot do. For example, a Black professor at a university asked for an unpaid leave of absence and was told that he was not eligible until six years of service. The professor read the personnel manual and found out that all professors are eligible for such leave after one full year of service to the university. Further, he found that the regulations required that he apply to the academic vice-president and that as long as he gained approval, he could renew such leave indefinitely, as long as he requested and received approval prior to June of the year before he wanted to be away.

Energy should not be expended trying to check the question of the racism involved or testing for the college administrator's lack of knowledge. The real issues here are that you were selected in an interview for the job, you were hired, and you are a new employee. Minorities and women who know the rules, regulations and guidelines then must discern what they mean and how they will be applied to them. Rather than examine the issue of race, minorities and women must remember that they are on probation. There may be no announced policy or terms for a probationary period, yet, as a new employee, you are on probation. Your supervisor may not speak to you of such a condition; nevertheless, you are on probation and will be treated as if you have probationary status no matter what your job title.

Getting the New Job

#44　　　**TOOL FOR SURVIVAL**　　　

Use your probationary period to learn the rules and regulations of the organization.

Try to ascertain what the consensus is on the length of the probationary period, even though there is no such written condition.

Ask questions rather than make statements, such as, "I would like clarification on this, please," or "Could you help me to understand this?," or "Did this cause that to happen?," or "What would happen if I were to attempt to . . .?"

When all else fails, "Go with the flow" for the first six months.

A great deal of time is spent helping the workers to understand organizational theory, the decision-making process, personnel policies and job classifications, and finance administration. Far too little time is spent on what to do after you get the job to ensure your survival.

Minorities and women must find some happy medium in which to take charge in their new job while exercising some restraints. First impressions are important and we all want ours to come across as personable, creative, intelligent, and productive. However, an excess of activity could turn off the very colleagues that you are trying to impress. Not even your superiors expect you to come in and to immediately take charge. You will need a few weeks and maybe a few months to conduct an intensive fact-finding mission. Susan Bodner of Estee Lauder Corporation says, "If you must assert yourself, do it by making contacts."[73] Remember, when you are new, even though you know the answers, it may not be your turn.

#45   TOOL FOR SURVIVAL

A few things to do while taking over a new job are:

1. Make sure you are formally introduced at the top level.

2. Introduce yourself to your peers.

3. Remember every peer is a potential subordinate or a potential boss.

4. Keep an open door so that those who want to can come learn about you.

5. Learn by listening. Information is power and you want to build as strong a power base as possible.

6. Measure the perimeters of your turf.

7. Learn the problem areas so that when the proper time comes you can put your skills to work to solve them.

8. Use noncommital positive-neutral responses such as, "Oh, I see, so that is how the budget works," or "Oh, yes, I've seen this issue before," or "Oh, I wonder how that will effect the organization?"

9. Develop the skill of nonjudgmental listening. You listen to gather information without agreement or disagreement.

10. Learn about problems in pursuit of a goal rather than in relation to the personalities involved. Stay out of the he-she game.[74]

A positive neutral stance is best, says career counselor Katherine Nash in her book *Get the Best of Yourself*. This means that you should listen to the opinions of others as you investigate who does what, where, and when in an organization. But the person to whom you are listening should go away feeling grateful that you took time out to listen.

#46   TOOL FOR SURVIVAL

You do not have any opinion as a new person on the staff.

Remember you are being checked out. The answers to the following questions leave important impressions:

1. Are you concerned about the organization?
2. Will your approach to tasks be positive or negative?
3. How will you demonstrate loyalty?
4. How will you use support?

No matter how relaxed the setting, no matter how informal the issue, no matter how friendly the team seems, minorities and women must be extremely careful about which issues they consider their own. "Work is work, and play is play and only with the gentlest discretion should the twain meet."[75] The basic two questions that could be used to determine whether or not you should consider this as an issue in which you want to become involved are:

1. Does the issue at hand directly involve me or significantly relate to my job or me as a worker?
2. How would my career be enhanced or damaged by my actions?

#47   **TOOL FOR SURVIVAL**

Unless you are directly involved, your job is significantly effected, or you are personally attached, do not take on or act on an issue as your own.

You might experiment with the answers to these questions:

1. Could the absence of any action taken by you improve the outcome?

2. Would the outcome truly be different if you did act?

3. Would you and your peers and co-workers suffer as a result of your action or lack of action?

While positive neutral stance is appropriate and effective for the new employee, professional assertivists are the workers who survive swimming with sharks over the long term. The risks are ever present:

"If you reach out to join the crowd, there's a chance you'll be cruelly rejected. If you speak up for all that you want and believe in, you bait the demoralization that accompanies a refusal. If you do your job exceedingly well, there's the strong possibility that some will respond with jealousy level resentment."[76]

Ambition is a fine characteristic for any worker. But ambition invites heartlessness and does not itself give back warmth and care. Minorities and women should weigh the risks of ambitious actions and should decide how much time and energy they might be willing to invest. Minority workers should take a reading about how much the actual return would be and whether the risks are worth the reward.

Career development and career empowerment are ongoing processes that provide tools for surviving while swimming with sharks in the world of work. Career development refers to the decisions about which areas to pursue for the development of skills that would augment one's ability to do a job. Black executives reported in the Wall Street Journal that prejudice still impedes their path to the top. The Journal article stated that Black workers are often too few in number and are assigned window-dressing posts.[77]

The corporate response to this allegation is that the development of people is a process that takes time. Walter Hoeppner, manager of personnel development for Standard Oil Company of Indiana, says, "Blacks did not even enter the corporate ranks until the late 1960's, so it takes anyone, Black or Caucasian, 15 to 25 years to rise to the top." However, Bernard Anderson, a Black economist with the Rockefeller Foundation, says that the "corporate culture," the combination of social contacts, corporate politicking, and technical knowledge make for successful Black workers in the labor market.

The three components for success: social contacts, corporate politicking, and technical knowledge, can all be increased by expanding the skill banks of minority workers. Minorities and women have been timid about developing skills in public speaking. Good public speaking skills are required to get on the career development ladder and those skills are mandatory if you are going to climb the organizational ladder. Also, math anxiety has hindered many minorities and women from developing technical knowledge. Minorities and women could seek the new curriculum of math, science, and technical knowledge. Lastly, the skills bank of the Black worker can be enhanced by seeking training for and entering non-traditional fields. Carol Tropp Schreiber found in her research of a large utilities company that those men and women who worked in transitional or cross-sex roles were happier than when they worked in traditional roles based on sex role stereotypes.

The following are some tools for building your skills bank:

#48   TOOL FOR SURVIVAL

Speak effectively.

> Outline what you want to say.

> Speak to everyone in the group.

> If you start to ramble—stop—consult your notes.

> Spontaneously enter conversations using a moderate tone of voice.

#49   TOOL FOR SURVIVAL

Write with impact.

> Remember to answer who, what, where, when, and how.

> List your main points in an outline.

> Place your main theme first.

> Tell your reader why what you have written is important.

> Rewrite any unclear points, any poorly worded phrases, and any details and ideas that have been omitted.

#50 TOOL FOR SURVIVAL

Express feelings without threats.

Give feedback in terms of your perceptions, such as, "I'm having some negative feelings about some things that you are doing," or "May I tell you how you come across to me?"

Only ask for acceptance of your feelings, not agreement. Try to understand the feelings of others before describing your own.

#51 TOOL FOR SURVIVAL

Listen effectively.

Exhibit patience.

Accept ideas with which you disagree; remain attentive.

Use responses to key messages so that you indicate your willingness to communicate on the agreed upon topics.

Listen for things of value to you and to your career.

Allow others to complete their thoughts.

Politics and Power

The use and understanding of politics and power are necessary for minorities and women to survive swimming with sharks in the world of work. Adele Scheele has said that the workforce is divided into *sustainers* who politely wait for recognition and reward and *achievers* who actually get that for which sustainers wait. Minorities and women have too often applied their skills and knowledge to their tasks and only become sustainers. Better application of politics and power can make achievers and survivors out of sustainers.

It takes months to actually size up the politics of your office and years to understand the politics of your organization. The effective use of office politics can mean the difference in being able to do your best work or not. A few tips for using office politics for the survival of female and minority workers are to:

1. Establish a good working relationship with secretaries. They are there to help you and can if you're not too proud to solicit help.
2. Befriend janitors and office managers. They can help to get your office in shape so that you look like you will be around awhile.
3. Your job is not the place where you go to win a popularity contest, but you must be friendly enough to get the job done well. Relax, smile, and be the you that is you.
4. If you make your job fun, you will have reserve energies that help you to tackle hard tasks.
5. Successful office politics are often called "lucky" happenings by female and minority workers. Remember that luck was once defined as that point in time when opportunity and preparation meet. Women and minorities must remember these factors about lucky people:[78]
   a. Lucky people are extroverted.
   b. Lucky people do their homework.
   c. Lucky people know the difference between a hunch and a hope.
   d. Lucky people are in touch with their feelings.
   e. Lucky people quit while they are ahead.
   f. Lucky people take risks.
   g. Lucky people admit mistakes.

The goal for minorities and women is to adopt and to exhibit the behaviors of lucky people, and to prepare for that point in time when the minority worker "gets lucky" or that time when opportunity and preparation meet.

#52   **TOOL FOR SURVIVAL**

Turn tokenism into a meaningful survival system.

Become extroverted, do your homework, get in touch with your feelings, take risks, admit your mistakes.

Get lucky. Get ready for that point in your career when both opportunity and preparation meet.

Power, power, who has the power? Traditional views of power indicate that power is a temporary condition, bestowed upon you by others, which comes from an external source and may be taken away without your consent. Since the Black worker is non-traditional in the paid labor force, any definition of power would necessarily be a non-traditional one. Therefore, power for minorities and women must come from an internal source, must have some permanence based on identified personal power, as based on personal issues, goals and targets.

Power for minorities and women is observed in those who survive the workforce sharks. The tenets in leadership as set forth by Simon and Presthus applied to Caucasian males; the body of knowledge called administration, as set forth by Getzels, applied to Caucasian females. The definitions of power delineated by Korda apply to any Caucasian male dominated organization. Minority workers who are powerful do not become immobilized, they do not commit suicide, they do not abuse drugs and alcohol, they do not perish from career burnout, they are survivors. They continue to walk, run, fall, skin their knees, brush off the gravel, get up again and again and continue to overcome. Minorities and women who survive redefine power. They are not willing to sell their souls, to compromise their principles, or to betray other workers in the name of upward mobility and advancement. Women and minorities "keep on keeping on" for the long term so that they can have food, shelter, loved ones, and so that they are alive to tell their stories as the powerful overcomers.

Minorities and women seldom own companies, yet they survive. Minorities and women seldom own tanks, guns, or other arsenals that represent traditional power, yet, they survive. Minorities and women do not own large profitable corporations, yet, they survive. Black workers have the most hazardous health histories, yet, they survive. Minority workers could not find enough cover in the universe to sufficiently cover themselves from attacks of blatant racism and bigotry on the job, yet, they survive. The backs of Black men, women and children in America were used to build the entire economic fibre of the country without the protection of law, life, or liberty, yet, they survived. Power, power, who has the power? Personal power, found in the spirit of the minority worker is the tool for survival.

#53   **TOOL FOR SURVIVAL**

Self-confidence initiates positive thought which motivates inner strength.

Positive thoughts about yourself create positive experiences which give you positive personal power.

The right clothes, a nice hair style, the right jewelry can foster positive thoughts about yourself.

"If you look good,
You feel good.
If you feel good,
You'll do good.
If you do good,
You'll practice good,
Then everything works together for good."

Martha's Creed

Personal Power

Self-confidence is a trait that must be learned in order to gain personal power. Since power truly is whatever you and other people perceive you to be able to accomplish, self-confidence is a key factor in building a power base.

#54   **TOOL FOR SURVIVAL**

Some confidence and power boosters:

> Set realistic goals that begin with and require one day at a time, one step at a time.

> Think positively about trial and error. Do not blame yourself for failure or try to avoid new challenges. Learn from each error and move on to new territory.

> Attract and associate with positive friends who encourage you.

> Work on your plans even when you change them along the way. You are growing and learning, so your plan will change.

> Build on each success. Toot your horn. Accept praise. Acknowledge your smallest accomplishments as successes.

> Use your successes as bridges to your next goal.

> Believe in yourself. Have faith in your personal power to survive.

Power and powerlessness are both affected by those who are your adversaries. Minorities and women sometimes lack access to accurate information about those who are their enemies. Some enemies come with your status as "new kid on the block." So there is no need to go beyond recognition that you have not provoked their antagonism. Others have sought the same position that you hold, and envy the power that you had to gain the job. Such people are eager to see you fail, and comment that your methods are wrong and you are incompetent.

There are enemies who may be above you but still see your competence as a threat to them. If you fail to turn them into allies, they will always do things to discredit you. It is this person that the minority worker should try to neutralize. Their "you're not going to show me up" attitude becomes troublesome and causes observable conflict. Your attempt to neutralize that conflict might include an attempt to indicate how your successes can in some ways make them look good. This usually fails because their attitudes and their responses are emotionally laden and highly irrational. You can feel certain that their attempts at sabotaging you will serve to discredit them. But you may find yourself in an ugly fight with a superior who is of the same race and/or sex that you are.

#55   TOOL FOR SURVIVAL

Know that if you find yourself involved in any problem that causes the organization to make a choice between you and one of your superiors, that is #1 and #2, #2, or the subordinate, always loses unless the top elite are ready to get rid of #1, your superior. So, never force this choice.

Remember, this tool holds sway even when you are right, even when #1 has been publicly and blatantly wrong, even when you can document the loss of profit directly or other embarrassment to the organization resulting from an error by #1.

#1 will always survive such an encounter, unless the organization has been ready to and is prepared to move #1 out.

Using Professional Assertivism

There are three ways to deal with or to handle political situations that directly and significantly involve the successful career patterns of minorities and women. They might:

1. Shrug off the situation so as not to raise it to an unwarranted level of importance, or
2. Ignore the situation by not accepting the incident as a personal affront, or
3. Act (and probably should) in a way that could be described as professional assertivism.

Two of your choices for action as a professional assertivist are: (1) to write a report, or (2) to write a memorandum. Both of these actions are political statements that represent both negative and positive risk-taking. Since written communications are political statements, you should give thought to the way they are prepared, and the way they will be received, as well as to how people will respond to them.

The report should adhere to the following principles for effective communications:

1. Involve your reader. Get the reader's interest with the first sentence.
2. Announce the structure of your report; that is, indicate that there will be a purpose, summary, findings, conclusion, and recommendations.
3. Separate fact from opinion. Remember that conclusions and recommendations are opinions.
4. Use an outline to guide you, taken from your notes.
5. State the facts fully and accurately. Use the 5 W's: who, what, when, where, why.
6. Interpret the facts. You may just set the record straight or you may attempt to set forth a plan for action.
7. Keep it short. Put supporting data in an appendix.
8. Visit the site of the office or place that you are talking about before you send your report.[79]

A model report uses its title to communicate its conclusions. An example of this was the report of the President's Commission on the

Accident at Three Mile Island. The report was entitled "The Need for Change: The Legacy of TMI."

In the business world, workers are encouraged to "get it in writing" or "to put it in writing." The memo has been used increasingly as the tool for such communication. Memos are used to help keep facts routinely on file, to serve as a ready reference, to use as recrimination, or to use as an offensive or defensive weapon. Because of the use of memos as a weapon, minority workers would be advised to consider memos as paper bullets.

Some quotes from other authors might help to underscore the point that all memos are political. Memos can be written to please, to push, or can serve as lethal weapons. Any memo can backfire in the hands of a novice. Linda J. Feurberg from the New York corporate-communications consulting firm says, "Like your clothes and hair style and the way you walk, memos project an image of who you are. Writing a memo is an art of illusion. You can create an atmosphere of power, or you can kill yourself."[80] Jane Trahey of a Chicago advertising firm states that, "Memos get by because they don't take the official role of a letter . . . . They're more informal and you can slip in things without people being aware of it. Memos can wreak havoc . . . ."[81] Jayne Townsend, who owns her own management training and consulting firm, says, "Notify, do not ask permission."[82]

Minorities and women could successfully use all of the advice of these authors with a slightly non-traditional plan. If you work in an organization where memos ricochet about, it is risky to join the fray. Marcia Orange, marketing program manager for Tektronix, Inc., of Portland, says, "Memos are overt, public, and permanent. Using them as a political tool is a sign of immaturity and lack of power."[83] Minorities and women may not survive a memo war.

TOOL FOR SURVIVAL

Ask forgiveness, do not ask permission.

Knowing where, and at whom, to aim a memo is not easy. Only experience teaches you. Every organization is different.

When in doubt, ask questions. Analyze memos of your predecessors.

If you decide that you must write a memo, leave out some things. That may give you maneuvering room if you need it later.

The quality of the business correspondence of minorities and women is in question because of the race and sex stereotype that presupposes, for example, that all Blacks lack English proficiency. Rely on your dictionary, your sense of what feels good to you, and a few standard rules.

#57   **TOOL FOR SURVIVAL**

1. Outline your format with a clear indication of to whom, from whom, and in regards to what in mind.

2. Clearly state the purpose of the memo.

3. Use a new paragraph for each main idea.

4. Check and double check for language, spelling, grammar, and sentence structure.

5. Watch your style and tone.

6. Be specific, businesslike, and to the point.[84]

Getting Fired: The Right Way

Anyone in the world of work, from entry level to executive, is likely to hear the words, "You're fired." The psychological pain for some has been so great as to, sometimes, be associated with death. Expressions like: "I got the ax," "I was canned," or "I was forced out," are commonly used to describe the ultimate corporate punishment, firing.

Every person reacts to being fired emotionally, physically, psychologically, and in other very personal ways. Some cry, some curse, some withdraw, some fall ill, and some people even cheer that it was the happiest day of their lives. Some firms have been established, whose major clientele includes counseling persons who have been fired. Other firms counsel employers about the dos and don'ts of proper ways to fire employees.

Accompanying the trauma related to finding another job, feelings of insecurity, anger, rejection, denial, and revenge, Black workers who survive need to get on with their lives. According to Jennifer Macleod, management consultant in New Jersey, "Long range career planning should include being prepared to be fired at least once, and perhaps several times in the course of a career."[85]

#58   **TOOL FOR SURVIVAL**

1. Keep up-to-date in your field. There is always a place for knowledge, skills, and talent.

2. Develop business contacts. Expand your contacts beyond mentors and friends to include former co-workers, business acquaintances, and conference attendees. Keep a card file.

3. Cultivate your sensitivity to the impending termination. If your career slows down, you receive written negative comments specific to your performance, you are refused budget and staff approval that you have strongly recommended, be aware.

4. Write and publish articles in professional journals. Establish yourself in publications. Know who might notice your work.

5. Use the same name throughout your career. Add names with marriage, but don't lose your professional identity.

6. Plan to negotiate your departure. Ask for time and salary until you gain new employment.

7. File *immediately* for unemployment benefits. You've earned them. They take the heat off so that you are not tempted to take an inferior and unwanted offer.[86]

Being prepared may be the key to a successful outcome as minorities and women move to the next stage in their careers. Even though a particular job and employer are no longer right for you, remember what Eleanor Roosevelt said, "No one can make you feel inferior without your consent." Use your feelings and your energies to get prepared.

Minorities and women could intensify their diversity for purposes of mobility and progress. That is, these workers should not have all of their career empowerment in any one basket. It is imperative to examine entrepreneurship even in a depressed economy for purposes of diversification. Entrepreneurs whose business efforts fail usually see themselves as one-dimensional, that is, with one area of specialization as their only earning power. Successful entrepreneurs are diversified for ease of response to customers, to the economy, and for their personal values and needs. For instance, a writer may write poems, feature stories, type theses for university students, and do typesetting in order to earn money. An artist may design dresses, do alterations, make dolls, make wooden toys and lamps for children's rooms, draw and paint, while she stays home raising her small son. If dress sales fall off, she has several activities to fall back on while she maintains her earning power.

Diversification does not mean going back to school to gain another degree. It does mean independent study and self-education.

Diversification may mean working with a friend or neighbor to gain new skills. Diversification may become a reality by enrolling in training courses that are offered by business, industry, or community groups. For example, if you would like to become a musician to increase your earning power, it may mean taking saxophone lessons. Another example is that diversification may mean buying a typing instruction book and renting a machine for the purpose of practicing and teaching yourself to type.

At the point at which you find yourself in a "must move" situation, minorities and women should view this as a positive opportunity for starting over. Some of the indicators of "must move" or "must start over" stituations are:

1. A termination date which is planned for after acquisition of funds and skills gained in a job where workers traditionally seek permanence;
2. Person did not gain salary increment or promotion;
3. Company policy changes demand that "Superspade" perform a "killer" task;
4. Job description revised directing the person to assume duties that have the deleterious effect of diminishing personal confidence levels.

You may plan to leave your permanent job. Planning may take the form of saving money during your last year or two of full-time employment. You must identify your marketable diversified skills that you would use to continue your earning power after you separate yourself from full-time employment. For example, a minority female may plan to have a child, and remain in the home until the child goes to school. She may operate a freelance secretarial service as a business from the home. She might also contract her services for two days weekly as a computer data entry clerk. She might substitute teach for a few days per week. She could enroll for training classes which teach technical and scientific courses. Several things are accomplished:

1. One recognizes one's continued earning power beyond a regular, full-time job;
2. One gains new skills for a time when one re-enters the workforce;

3. One increases personal power and decreases dependence on traditional full-time employment.

Minorities and women have earning power beyond their jobs. They have skills that can be marketed to earn money. For instance, minorities and women who organize kitchen shelves when putting away groceries have a skill transferable to a job called grocery shelving clerk or shelf stocker.

If minority workers find themselves without a job, they must remember that they still have earning power. In order to start over, one must assess one's skills in order to determine how to operationalize personal earning power. We interviewed a minority female computer specialist, who was forced to quit her job when her supervisor asked her to add cleaning the men's toilets and emptying the trash cans to her job description. There was the choice of adding these tasks to her duties or leaving to start over. This woman chose leaving her job, because to stay had the effect of reducing her personal power, taking away her self-confidence, and raising her personal stress beyond healthy levels.

#59   **TOOL FOR SURVIVAL**

DIVERSIFY!

You really can do more than one thing in a lifetime.

Divert your talents and skills into many areas in order to increase your earning power and to enhance your personal power.

Try some non-traditional combinations like computer specialist and bartender. Part-time professor and gas station attendant, seamstress and data entry clerk, student and lawn service employee are other examples of combinations.

Diversity provides a fall back position which maintains your earning power.

Turning Point

Clarke and McCarty say that getting fired can become a turning point rather than a dead end.[87]

#60   **TOOL FOR SURVIVAL**

Give yourself time to examine and to deal with all of the feelings that accompany firing.

Ask yourself whether or not you actually:

1. Lost status?

2. Lost a position that you needed?

3. Lost a position that you wanted?

4. Were willing to work that hard for that little reward?

5. Were willing to work those long hours with so little personal time left?

6. Were confusing antagonism with strength and power?

7. Were engaged in a self-defeating predicament, while your every effort only further alienated persons whose cooperation was vital to your work?

Sometimes a third party is helpful to assist you to examine what you have experienced. Embarrassment, withdrawal, depression, and rejection make rational thinking very difficult. Friends, relatives, or a therapist would be helpful if they knew some of the facts related to the situation, but had not been in any way personally involved. The most important characteristic of the third party intervening would be the ability to assist the minority worker to highlight and to build on personal strengths.

Legal leverage may be the order of the day as you decide to get started again. The Equal Employment Opportunities Commission is the agency established to enforce equal pay for equal work, and that equal benefits be afforded to both males and females regardless of race, color, creed, or age. Two words of advice, if you decide to use legal leverage.

#61   **TOOL FOR SURVIVAL**

Look for other employment while your charge is pending in EEOC. Also, get legal advice from your own attorney.

Pay your bills and make no new purchases. You may be without the benefit of your regular income for two years or more.

Consider "being fired" as time out to look at dreams that have been deferred too long, personal needs that have been on hold, and compromises that you were forced to make against your better judgment. This may be just the time to take some essential time out. Being out of work may be a good time to determine whether or not you really have what it takes to be self-sufficient. Not having to go to a job may give just the time to cool out and to recognize your true likes and dislikes. For example, one Black male thought that his heart's desire was to live in suburbia. He had grown up in a large, midwestern, densely-populated city. When he was fired and no longer had to commute three hours per day, he realized that he loved the city. He had become involved in activities in the urban center that had nothing to do with his job. He was commuting back to the city for evening engagements during the week. Also, he spent time commuting to the city on weekends to visit Black friends. He sold his suburban home in the predominantly Caucasian community, moved to the city, and at last check, had absolutely no regrets. Also, surprisingly, he reported that he had found no reason to even visit the suburban town.

Public policy issues, a depressed economy, neoracism, and neosexism have caused many circumstances in which large numbers of minorities and women are in the ranks of the unemployed. Some of them were laid off or fired.

Minorities and women could apply new, unique, and non-traditional tools to solve earning power challenges. A new, unique, and non-traditional tool is one called creative budgeting. Traditionally, the phrase "necessity is the mother of invention" has been applied to explain the basis of this tool. However, effective use by minorities and women of the term creative budgeting is defined as development of innovative, tactical strategies for fulfilling financial needs. For example, a Black male with a Ph.D. became unexpectedly unemployed with only two weeks' severance pay and twenty-six weeks of unemployment benefits. His income had been above $40,000.00. He used the tool "creative budgeting" to restore his earning power. He sought three different kinds of part-time employment. He gained a part-time teaching job; he contracted himself as a consultant; and he pumped gas on weekends. The key to creative budgeting is to decide what your true financial needs are, such as food, rent, and heat. Then, "Go for it!" "Go for it" means do what has to be done to survive. Maybe, this tool should be used doing things that represent another turning point, such as leaving the public sector for private sector employment. Creative budgeting as a tool could mean turning from white collar to blue collar employment goals. The high level of minority youth unemployment is a tragedy when one finds that lawn services are largely operated and owned by Caucasian males.

#63   **TOOL FOR SURVIVAL**

Use creative budgeting to survive.

Determine the true level of your financial needs for survival, that is, food, shelter, utilities, and transportation.

Then, examine your skills bank to discover money-making ideas.

If you need money, go get it!

Making It On Your Job

Workers make every effort to keep their options open in order to enjoy mobility, choices, and changes in the workplace. One of the worker's choices is to stay on the job and to make the experience a positive one. Making it on your present job is sometimes a career decision that takes great courage and is seldom an easy choice. Therefore, an operating plan is most necessary in order to successfully remain on your job.

Because you have some history and background about the people and the politics where you work, you should probably start out to determine which elements you can accurately predict. Your predictability quotient should have a high positive correlation to your level of involvement and time spent in your present position. Your access to accurate information and people who are considered significant others in the organization would also be most helpful.

There are some tools for survival that would be appropriate to implement when you've made the commitment to stay on your job. Remember that people in your work environment will be aware that you are digging in and that you are ready for long term goal setting. There may or may not be some resistance to your decision. Just be aware that you don't have to make any announcement to co-workers for them to pick up on your new energy. The discussion of the following "Tools" is provided in order to assist the reader to design an operating plan for finding success on the job. Take a reading of your comfort level during professional interactions as well as during informal ones on your job. Record these readings in a journal that is kept hidden away from all eyes at home. Read your recordings at least once monthly. Note changes and make mental notes of behaviors and situations that caused you to experience higher levels of discomfort.

Adjust your approaches, behaviors, and responses to situations based on your comfort levels. For example, if you note three arguments in the teacher's lounge during the month, you might decide to go out to lunch and to use the student's bathroom. If your secretary takes you through a fire drill of concerns each time you return to the office from visits to the field, have a talk before you leave about your need to have some problem solving done while you're away. Then take notes and make no comments at your meeting with the secretary when you return. Take care of the issues in a calm and determined manner. Try not to share in the fire drill.

#64   **TOOLS FOR SURVIVAL**

Take a reading of your comfort level. Record your rating and the contributing behaviors. Nothing is really solved by sharing and struggling with the discontent of others. Then, adjust your response and behaviors. Calm, poised and easy does it!

Female mid-level managers reported that they found a great deal of hostility in conversation patterns between themselves and their male supervisors. These patterns were the same when examined for race and ethnic differences. The frequency of these reports caused the investigation. The following examples represent introductory conversations initiated by male supervisors and some of the traditional female responses:

Male	Female
1. I hope you won't be too sensitive about this, but . . .	1. Oh, this sounds serious
2. Don't take this personally, but . . .	2. Oh dear, what have I done?
3. I know that you don't want to hear this, but . . .	3. Everyone here is grown, let's have it.
4. I don't want to discuss this now, but I need to tell you . . .	4. Well, I'm glad you told me what is troubling you.

Workers should be able to capitalize on the investment in their careers. In order to transform the worker's time, planning, and dedication into money for personal resources, males and females must converse using healthy and balanced motives.

Some of the hostility in the traditional exchanges can be traced to stereotypes held about male/female communications. Research shows that there are some commonly held misconceptions that must be overcome.

1. Men mean business when they talk while women's voices are not authoritative.
2. The powerful speak while the powerless listen. A 1979 study found that women introduce more possible topics for conversation but topics introduced by men, while fewer in number, were highly successful as topics of conversation.
3. Broadcasters are mainly Caucasian males in their 30's and 40's; only one in 20 is non-white; only one in 5 is female; one in 12 is following a father who was a journalist because people do not take women seriously.
4. Men are less talkative than women. However, in a 1975 study of talkativeness using descriptions of pictures, men spoke for thirteen (13) minutes while women spoke for only three (3) minutes.

Research indicates that listeners regardless of sex are more likely to interrupt and to disagree with a female speaker than a male speaker. These factors cause men and women to have problems in business discussions and to experience dislocations in conversation on the job.

We have field tested the following responses and found that they motivate more positive interactions. In some cases, we observed that the male supervisors really heard the remark for the first time when it was repeated verbatim by the female. Some males completely dropped these conversational patterns from their repertoire.

#65   TOOLS FOR SURVIVAL

1. I hope you won't be too sensitive about this, but . . .

    1. Everyone knows that I am sensitive, so just carefully say whatever you must say.

2. Don't take this personally but . . .

    2. You are talking to me, a person, so what are you saying when you state "don't take this personally."

3. I know that you don't want to hear this, but . . .

    3. You're right, I don't want to hear this, so let's skip this one.

4. I don't want to discuss this now, but I need to tell you . . .

    4. I don't mean to interrupt, but why don't we wait until you do want to discuss this matter.

These responses are different from the troublesome exchanges in two important ways. First, the responses suggested as "tools" place both parties in positions of taking responsibility for their words. No one party could step out into the role of spectator. Secondly, both parties become aware that there must be agreement to discuss a topic before any communication can take place.

According to Betty Lehan Harragan, author of *Knowing the Score*, the most obvious indicator of inadequate gamesmanship is pervasive dissatisfaction or apprehension about your job. Harragan states, that a job should be "more fulfilling than aggravating, more engrossing than bewildering, more absorbing than frustrating, and more hopeful than discouraging." [88]

Women today have some special kinds of problems on the job. Most particularly do ambitious women experience problems on the job. One of the problems that women experience is a result of any challenge to the position, place, or restrictive slot into which they've been placed. Some very ambitious women have looked back over their challenges during the 80's and have determined that when a problem is identified some action is necessary. However, they reported that their actions have been modified from a direct confrontation based on some rules, regulations, or guidelines to maneuvers that are in a constant state of flux. These women report that they've begun to pay attention to the use of feminine beauty, and finesse. While this sounds like a move back to something once called female maneuvering, it could be said that women have refined use of their skills and talents. In any struggle, the parties involved search for tools that bring success. Success means doing what works.

#66   TOOLS FOR SURVIVAL

Be your own feminine self.

Refine those things that you love about being a woman. Chances are others love you for them too.

Acknowledge the beauty of your mind, body and spirit.

Do whatever works! Victory is sweet, joyfilled and pleasant.

Managing Stress and Career Burnout

Barbara Hojad

CHAPTER FIVE

CHAPTER FIVE

"A diamond was never made unless some pressure was put on it."

Anonymous

Managing Stress and Career Burnout

Many changes have taken place in the world of work. Some of the new phenomena have been the result of the world of politics, the politics of oil, social changes, economic changes, and population changes. The workplace has inherited a younger, more affluent, better educated cadre of workers, which has created some conflicts causing great stress in organizations. Some of the stressors resulting from changes in the workplace are talked about in Toffler's book, *The Third Wave*, in which he describes a need for workers with highly technical, scientific, highly computerized and mechanized skills. However, another set of factors causing conflict is that more minorities and women are entering the labor market, having no children, seeking advancement, remaining single longer, and taking no time out as they pursue their careers. The impact of the race and sex factors has caused conflict and stress in the workplace.

The clashing of different backgrounds has caused stress for both the minority and dominant groups. Caucasian males have previously enjoyed homegeneous work settings. The labor market has changed very quickly into a more heterogeneous place. Competition has reached very high levels between males and females, and between minorities and majorites, as barriers were removed to entry-level positions and as some obstacles were removed to managerial positions. The phrase "reverse discrimination," as adopted by Caucasian males, was a response to some of the structural changes in the work force.

Perceptions in the dominant culture included mental sets for accepting minorities and women as dead-ended workers, and Caucasian males as upwardly mobile and managers. Organizational hierarchies reinforced such perceptions. So as Black workers moved beyond those perceptions, people who were unaccustomed to changes in the hierarchy and shared power, created conflict that produced stress. A Black female that we interviewed related the story about her staff of three Caucasian males, one Caucasian female professional, and two Caucasian female secretaries. Within the organization it was considered acceptable behavior for the staff to use such communications as "Yes, ma'am, what you say, boss lady," "You only say that because you don't like Caucasians very much anyway." The secretaries responded to any request for folders or messages, "Yes, ma'am, Miss Scarlet." When the Black female reported these comments to her supervisor and asked for assistance to explain that these statements were racial slurs, she was asked, "Why are you so sensitive about being Black?"

The Black supervisor went to plan X and tried professional assertivism. She scheduled private conferences with each staff member, discussed a written operational plan for project tasks, and provided a suggested format for evaluation of each person's progress. She was removed from her position and told that such a plan of operation had been assessed as coming from a heartless, insensitive person. She was told that, since she could not improve the way that the Caucasian staff felt about her, she had rendered herself ineffective as a supervisor. She was demoted, moved to another project, at a loss of $3300 in salary. She had struggled to bring stability to the staff for six months. She had asked three levels up the chain of command for assistance. Each one of the Caucasian males indicated that he saw no problem, other than the lack of inter-personal skills of the Black supervisor. However, the demotion, move, and loss of salary were done during the first fifteen minutes on one Monday morning. When the Black supervisor protested that no investigation had been made, and that there was no logic to the hasty retreat, she was told that she was lucky to have a job at all. "You know we did you a favor not to fire you."

Fernandez refers to a time bomb that could go off any minute if it continues to be ignored. The time bomb is loaded with stressors from conflicts between managers' views regarding equal employment opportunity and affirmative action programs. For example, in many organizations, new promotional policies have resulted in young educated Black workers supervising older, less educated Caucasian males. Many older workers have become subordinates as younger workers become their managers. This causes great difficulty and conflict. [89]

142

Kathryn Weld, in her examination of stereotypes vs. reality, and limits vs. potential, refers to the inadequate management of stress and the effects of the new conflicts:

". . . hidden conflict can also be reflected in tardiness and absenteeism, high turnover and production errors; increased accidents, grievances, and transfer requests; plus decreased productivity. In addition, there are stress related physical symptoms: insomnia, headache; hypertension, asthma; and cardiac irregularities; weight changes; ulcers and colitis; uncontrolled use of drugs, cigarettes, and food; anxiety and depression. These all suggest unresolved conflict in the workplace and add to occupational burnout." [90]

Job stress and burnout can originate from problems related to the environment. Most full-time workers spend at least 2,000 hours per year at the job site. Since many Black workers work in service, entry-level, and janitorial type jobs, there are three problems for which they should be especially on guard:

1. Poor ventilation—not enough fresh air is circulated in sealed buildings. This can cause drowsiness, respiratory problems, and infections.
2. Carcinogenic agents—cancer causing agents, such as asbestos, have especially been found dangerously exposed in schools, factories, and office buildings.
3. Noise pollution—some legal limits have been set restricting high noise levels that could cause permanent damage to the ear, as well as nervous conditions.

Stress and Its Effects

A number of medical scientists believe stress is the basic cause of many diseases. Stress research dates back to the 1930's when attempts were made to determine what characteristics in people cause such things as heart attacks. Research conducted by the federal government, particularly research done by the military on servicemen and women during war or threat of war, indicates that serum cholesterol, blood sugar, and blood pressure rise extremely high during periods of stress.

Dr. Hans Selye, long considered the father of stress research, defines stress as the "non-specific response of the body to any demand made on it."[91] He goes on to say that the initial response to any kind of stress is alarm. This is followed by the stage of resistance, a chemical rallying of the body's defenses. If the alarm or threat is continued over a long period of time, the individual's resources are exhausted. The defense system wears down. The body can no longer adapt to the demand.

Dr. Selye refers to this response process as the "general adaptation syndrome." Once an individual's adaptation energy has been expended, there is no known way to replenish it. Selye likens a person's supply of "adaptation energy" to a nation's deposits of oil: once it has been summoned up and burned, it is gone, and the individual goes shortly thereafter.

Stress is caused by life change events—events that require readjustments or getting used to. Stressful events (also known as stressors) may be pleasant (eustress) or unpleasant (distress). When we refer to stress in a negative sense, we are talking about distress. Uncertainty and strangeness are stressful because they threaten our safety, lifestyle, and beliefs. Expectation of a stressful event can be as strong a stressor as the event itself. One's perception of a life change is the important factor in determining the degree of stress. A change may mean one thing to one individual and something else to another. Everyone is always under some degree of stress, even when asleep.

Stress is not necessarily bad. Though stressors may be different from or opposite each other (pleasant or unpleasant), the non-specific demand to adjust or adapt may be the same. In other words, a situation need not be damaging to be stressful. A kiss may cause the same amount of stress as a slap in the face. So, some stress is good for us as long as we are able to manage it. When stress gets out of control, it becomes dangerous and often leads to a major crisis.

Many stressful events are beyond our control, but we can control how we respond to those events. For example, we cannot control other people's behavior, but we can control how we react to that behavior. The control and reaction factors are what we will be most concerned about as we try to manage stress.

How We Create Stress

LIFESTYLE

We live in a competitive society where we define winners and losers, causing people-top-people threats. Threats bring on stress. Technology, present almost everywhere, threatens us. New-found freedoms for women, children, and racial minorities bring new responsibilities, and this threatens everyone. People long for the opportunity to be creative, but creativity is not always welcome in an industrial society. The jet age that implies we must hurry, get where we need to go, fast, do what we need to do, fast, causes us to rush when there is no need to. Our governments, our values, our needs and desires have all changed, and change is threatening. Any change brings about stress.

VALUES AND BELIEFS

Conflicting values and beliefs create stress. When we attempt to let go of values instilled in us over many years and assume new values that may be popular, tensions begin to build from within. An example: If a teacher supports sex education because other teachers do, but secretly opposes birth control, there is a conflict in values, causing stress. One should commit oneself to one particular value as being more important than another.

Selye suggests that one major source of stress arises from a "dissatisfaction with life," and more specifically from "disrespect for one's own accomplishments." [92] Most people find that a little success in life will help tremendously. People want life to make a statement; when it does not, a feeling of worthlessness may develop, bringing on stress. Because this stress-inducing society places so much emphasis on ambition and status, acquisitions such as money, power, and recognition give us a sense of worth and free us from much distress. When individuals are not able to achieve success by society's standards, they must define their own standard of success by creating a worthwhile purpose in life and striving for it. For example, many people who are convinced of and who believe in the power of religion seem to live a less stressful life than others who do not hold such beliefs.

REACTIONS TO EVENTS

We create stress by our reactions to stressful events. Behavior patterns dictate those reactions, which means that some people handle stress better than others.

McQuade and Aikman discuss aggressive and dependent behaviors as ways to get what we feel we need in life.[93] While all of us use both aggressive behavior and dependent behavior, some people are mainly aggressive and others mainly dependent. "Dependency and constructive aggression can work together. Dependency and hostility (destructive aggression) only get in each other's way and produce anxiety."

Behaviors can be emotionally "nourishing" or emotionally "toxic," according to Jerry Greenwald.[94] He describes how one can minimize unnatural (toxic) behavior and emphasize the natural (nourishing) behavior. He says, "No matter how awful the situation, you are the most capable person to do something about it." Toxic behavior (pain, suffering, anxiety, tension) is necessary at times, but we have to be able to determine when it is not necessary.

Donald Tubesing describes people who exhibit excessive competitive drive, aggressiveness, impatience, and a sense of time urgency as having "Type A" behavior.[95] "People who engage in this type of behavior," he says, "are always in struggles with everyone and everything including themselves." Tubesing suggests "Type B" behavior as being the more relaxed way of life. Society rewards Type A behavior and most jobs are set up in this manner, he says. On the other hand, people who exhibit Type B behavior do not put all their worth into succeeding at a task. Type B reflects what life should be about.

When we react to a stressful event, we need to consider:

1. Do I have control or is the control in the hands of someone else?
2. Is this worth dealing with? In other words, am I spending $10 worth of adrenalin on a 10¢ problem?
3. Is it important to achieving my life or professional goals?
4. Is attempting to deal with the event more stressful than the event itself?
5. Are the benefits greater than the energy I will have to expend?

We generally react to stress in two ways: (1) fight (or attack), and

(2) flight (or retreat). Occasionally we react by standing fast, but this in a sense is the same as retreating. Ancient peoples reacted instinctively to threats or alarms by attacking or retreating. Animals still react in this manner. Twentieth century lifestyles prohibit us from reacting instinctively to the various threats we face each day. We react in other ways—physically and internally. More often than not, our fighting goes on internally and often our flights or retreats are retreats in behavior only; attitudinally they are fights, carried on internally.

Medical scientists tell us that these continuous physical reactions damage the circulatory system, digestive tract, lungs, muscles, and joints, and hasten the process of aging.

What Stress Does to Health

Stress saps the energy. People with little energy are susceptible to all kinds of diseases. "It is not only a matter of insufficient sleep, it has been proven that stress actually disturbs the immunological system itself."[96] Stress causes problems in:

1. The cardiovascular system, which can lead to:

     a. Heart Attacks
     b. Hypertension
     c. Angina
     d. Arrhythmia
     e. Migraine

2. The digestive system and related organs, which can lead to:

     a. Ulcers
     b. Colitis
     c. Constipation
     d. Diarrhea
     e. Diabetes

3. The immunological system, which can lead to:

     a. Infections
     b. Allergies
     c. Cancer

4. The skeletal-muscular system, which can lead to:
    a. Backache
    b. Tension headache
    c. Arthritis
    d. Accident proneness.

Tubesing examines stress in relation to the whole person and his/her health and illness (the *Holistic Model of Health and Illness*).[97] He suggests that five aspects of life should be examined for their health or illness to determine the health of the individual: physical, intellectual, spiritual, emotional, and social. Each aspect, he says, is a separate measure or system, and illness in any one area can affect another area, causing illness in that area also. One must look at the symptoms, causes, and treatments in each of these areas to make the whole person well.

Performance Symptoms

TARDINESS

Tardiness rarely is an accident. Tardiness often is rooted in unconscious feelings about your job or something else in your life. Some of those feelings are:
1. Boredom—your present job does not satisfy your career goals—lateness is your way of expressing resistance to spending your valuable time at the office.
2. Anxiety—your supervisor, co-workers, or job tasks make you insecure—lateness is your way of saying no to an uncomfortable situation.
3. Resentment—Authority displeases you—lateness is your way of getting control. You need to be a free spirit, and you need total freedom to come and go as you choose.

DECLINING PERFORMANCE

Quite often declining work performance can be traced to the fact that a person's personal problems have invaded the workplace. Several clues to this problem are:
1. You begin to "act" like you are working. Even if you work longer hours, you get less done.
2. Your concentration is poor.

3. Your sense of time is distorted; the hours drag on.
4. Your relationships dramatically change. Those around you start to fall into two groups—those against you, and those for you. Everything at work becomes personalized.

CHRONIC COMPLAINING

Change is one of the chief causes of chronic complaining. People like the known, and any change is viewed as stressful and conflictual. There are several other contributors to chronic complaining:
1. The way people treat one another's ideas and views.
2. A perception of being unfairly treated, not given due recognition, or being moved around arbitrarily.
3. A need to "win" in spite of immeasurable obstacles, i.e., a confrontation with your supervisor.

Solutions for Stress Problems

An individual may determine solutions for stress problems by the degree of excess stress he/she is experiencing. Though there is no one procedure for relieving a stressful situation, many well-known helpers such as diet, exercise, or slowing down are suggested frequently. One of the best ways to manage stress is to understand it and how it affects people and then apply this to your own situation. Doing this will help you find better ways to solve your own problems.

Work hard in life at something that interests you and that you are good at. The aim of life is self-expression, an aim usually difficult to fulfill in our society. — Hans Selye

Stress Buildup

Excess stress is one of the biggest causes of burnout. It overloads your circuits and saps your energy. Since most people don't have circuit breakers, the indications of too much stress are chronic headaches, ulcers, heart disease, and job burnout.

The following test, Social Readjustment Rating Scale, developed by two Seattle physicians. T. H. Holmes and R.H. Rahe, can give you an indication of the amount of stress you are under.[98] Add up the points in parentheses for each of the questions that applies to you.

In the last year you have had a:

1. ____ Death of spouse (100)
2. ____ Divorce (73)
3. ____ Marital separation (65)
4. ____ Jail term (63)
5. ____ Death of close family member (63)
6. ____ Personal injury or illness (53)
7. ____ Marriage (50)
8. ____ Fired at work (47)
9. ____ Marital reconciliation (45)
10. ____ Retirement (45)
11. ____ Change in health of family member (44)
12. ____ Pregnancy (40)
13. ____ Sex difficulties (39)
14. ____ Gain of new family member (39)
15. ____ Business readjustment (39)
16. ____ Change in financial state (39)
17. ____ Death of a close friend (37)
18. ____ Change to different line of work (36)
19. ____ Change in number of arguments with spouse (35)
20. ____ Mortgage over $10,000 (31)
21. ____ Foreclosure of mortgage or loan (30)
22. ____ Change in responsibilities at work (29)
23. ____ Son or daughter leaving home (29)
24. ____ Trouble with in-laws (29)
25. ____ Outstanding personal achievement (28)
26. ____ Wife begin or stop work (26)
27. ____ Begin or end school (26)
28. ____ Change in living conditions (25)
29. ____ Revision of personal habits (24)
30. ____ Trouble with boss (23)
31. ____ Change in work hours or conditions (20)
32. ____ Change in residence (20)
33. ____ Change in schools (20)
34. ____ Change in recreation (19)
35. ____ Change in church activities (19)
36. ____ Change in social activities (18)
37. ____ Mortgage or loan less than $10,000 (17)
38. ____ Change in sleeping habits (16)
39. ____ Change in number of family get-togethers (15)
40. ____ Change in eating habits (15)
41. ____ Vacation (13)
42. ____ Christmas (13)
43. ____ Minor violations of the law (11)

_____ Total

What does your score mean?   Total score
                               150-199 Mild life crisis
                               200-299 Moderate life crisis
                               300 +   Major life crisis

Managing Stress: Tool for Survival

A. YOUR VALUES AND LIFE GOALS

1. Recognize your limitations. Do your best on a task and don't feel guilty if you don't reach perfection.
2. Be honest with yourself about why you continue in a stressful situation. For example: If your job is just a meal ticket for you, admit it to yourself. Don't try to convince yourself or others that you are in this job because you enjoy it when the truth is you do this kind of work because you are being paid to do so.
3. If you are having difficulty achieving a goal or completing a task, don't waste time feeling like a failure. Move on to another goal or task.
4. Don't give all of yourself to anything or anyone without getting something for you. To do this is not unselfishness; it is rational selfishness.
5. Identify stressful events that you can control and let go of those over which you have no control.
6. Remove yourself from the "toxic" people and contaminated environments in your life. You don't need them, whether they are supervisors, colleagues, friends, or the happy hour crowd.

B. YOUR CONTROL OF TIME

1. Organize your time by dividing tasks into three categories:
   a. Those tasks that are important to achieving your life or professional goals.
   b. Those tasks that are important to other people or tasks that you just want to do.
   c. Tasks that are not important to your life or professional goals and you don't really want to do them at all.

Always start with a, then b if time permits, c is always last, and chances are you won't have to do them at all.

2. Don't allow others or insignificant events to waste even 10 minutes of your time.

3. Learn to say no.

C. YOUR ATTITUDE

1. You can change your attitude toward a stressful event by redefining the event. For example: If you usually get upset when your supervisor unnecessarily exerts her/his authority because you find this demeaning, redefine the supervisor's behavior as being a self-induced boost to her/his insecurity.

2. Consider yourself number one in your life as long as your actions are not harmful to others.
   a. Be friends with yourself.
   b. Act and react based on your needs as you define them and not on what others expect your needs to be.
   c. Develop the I/me syndrome. How do I feel today? What is good for *me*? What do *I* need and want for *me*?

3. Surround yourself with people who make you feel good and whom you help to feel good.

D. SPIRITUAL OUTLOOK

1. If you have strayed away from your religious beliefs, find some form of spiritual renewal.
2. Practice strengthening your faith through prayer and meditation.
3. Study about others who have found new meaning in their lives by making spiritual commitments.

E. HEALTH, DIET, AND EXERCISE

1. Consider drastically changing your eating habits. Investigate the benefits of macrobiotic and vegetarian diets.
2. Search for and find physical activities that do not require others or special equipment. Do them regularly. Vary your exercise. Combine in one week yoga, swimming, walking, and biking.
3. Develop breathing exercises that decrease stress.
4. Have your physician help you to rule out medical causes of your stress. [99]

[99] Adapted from *Survival of Stressed Teachers* by Jesse Muse, NEA, 1980.

Treatments for Career Burnout

The following are some guidelines for reducing stress:

1. Very few people will understand what you're doing; therefore, it becomes an exercise in futility to judge yourself completely by others' standards. This includes your friends, the public, and in a limited sense, your peers.
2. During your career you must decide what is morally right and wrong for you, and determine if your views agree with or are in conflict with organizational codes and policies.
3. It is extremely important that any person be able to account for his or her actions and be able to accept and cope with the consequences, whether they are fair or unfair; whether you like them or not.
4. Above all, it is necessary to be truthful with yourself. Assume that your job will affect every aspect of your life, particularly family and/or social life. Many times the effects will be adverse and the degree of adversity will depend upon your flexibility to unusual circumstances.

The following are some guidelines for managing Career Burnout:

There is a famous cartoon in which two men are shown chained to a stone wall. One is whispering to the other, "And now for Plan B."

Managers without a Plan B limit themselves to a single option. Those with a Plan B train themselves to consider many options even if they don't immediately make a move. If you have a feasible Plan B, you're likely to be much more highly motivated to do better work in your present situation and to avoid stress and career burnout.

Here are four possible solutions for your need for a Plan B.

1. JOB SCRAMBLER

This term describes a person who has something to offer, something valuable that another organization wants—specialized knowledge, creative ideas, innovative systems or leadership. Sometimes the scrambler's tangible asset appears intangible (a "feel" for hiring, a good "gut" about market, an undefinable something), but the intangible must, in fact, be there even if it can't be readily located.

2. LATERAL TRANSFER

A lateral transfer is designed to broaden the knowledge base and abilities of the employee while at the same time providing the employer with a trained pool of talent which can reduce the cost of replacing persons who get promoted or retire.

3. PROFESSIONAL SELF-RENEWAL

Renewal means to make effective, to restore or replenish for an additional period. Thus professional self-renewal would mean that you, the individual, would take steps to update your formal education, would attend and participate in your professional association meetings. Professional self-renewal could also mean that you investigate the possibilities of getting into a field that has long interested you. This second field could serve as a source of pleasure and release from your job.

4. JOB ROTATION

Job rotation is a temporary move designed to expose competent, capable employees to other areas of their company. As employees become more senior in their positions, they look to promotion as a method of realizing their potential. If there is a log-jam at the supervisory level in one's primary job area, disapppointment and dissatisfaction can result. By rotating employees among divisions and areas, the employer helps to reduce frustration, raise moral support and provide the company with a cadre of multi-trained employees.

Techniques For Overcoming Stress

RELAXATION

In order to live happy, fulfilling lives, we must be able to approach life with vitality and enthusiasm. To do this we need to become balanced and in harmony with our surroundings and ourselves. One basic concept to understand in order to achieve this goal is relaxation.

Our view of relaxation is often "getting away from it all"—for example, going to the mountains, playing tennis, or going on a vacation. However, true relaxation is the cessation of activity. The dictionary defines relaxation as abatement or remission, diminution of tension. What we learn to do is stop! What happens?

Our mind becomes quiet, our body rests, and our breath becomes even and deep. This is relaxation. How do we do this? The first step is to sit quietly.

1. Lie on your back or sit comfortably, hands to the side, palms down, eyes closed.
2. While breathing normally, bring the awareness to the breath. Notice the flow of the breath, the rising and falling of the chest.
3. Scan the body looking for any area of tension or tightness and breathe into that area, using the breath to release the tension.
4. Visualize the mind as a large body of water as far as the eye can see. Imagine tensions or stress as waves on the water. As the mind becomes quieter, the waves become smaller until the water is still and calm.
5. Begin to relax the body by allowing a deep sense of relaxation to move into each body part. Begin with the feet and move very slowly up the legs, through the abdomen, hands and arms, neck, head, face, then lungs and heart. Using the breath, feel, on the inhalation, a warm tingling sensation enter the area; on the exhalation, feel the breath carry all tension and tightness away.
6. Once completely relaxed, begin to bring the awareness back to the physical body and stretch. Try to maintain this same sense of relaxation as long as possible.

Whenever feeling tense, simply allow this visualization to come to mind for a few minutes, using it to calm and refresh you.

THE BREATH

We breathe approximately 21,600 times a day, but do we really notice *how* we breathe? If we notice our breath, we will begin to see its connection with the mind and emotions. When agitated, the breath becomes rapid, the pulse is elevated. This is the beginning of a stressful situation. By controlling the breath, we are able to begin to deal effectively with the mind and emotions.

By slowing and deepening the breath, we are becoming sensitive to what is taking place within our mind and body. By continually reevaluating our emotional and mental condition, we are releasing the tensions which plague us. What does this breath sensitivity do for us?

Physically, our blood pressure is lowered, the nerves are soothed, allowing us to become more *relaxed* in our attitude. Through this process we are able to approach our work, relationships, and our lives in a more objective and sensitive way.

USING THE BREATH

1. Become aware of your breathing during stressful situations.
2. Are *you* controlling your mind?

COMPLETE BREATH

1. Relax abdominal muscles; focus the attention on the abdomen.
2. Inhaling, expand abdominal muscles, then rib cage, inhaling to the top of the lungs, just below the collarbone.
3. Hold breath for an instant.
4. Exhale slowly, making sure to completely empty the lungs.
5. Taking no breaths in between, begin the complete breath again.

Purpose: 1) Brings awareness to the breath, 2) Increases oxygen flow to the brain, helping to clear the mind, 3) Fosters relaxation.

WATCHING THE BREATH

1. Breathe normally
2. Bring the attention to the breath
3. Notice the rising and falling of the chest
4. Listen to the sound of the breath
5. As the mind wanders, continue to bring the attention back to the breath
6. Remember to breathe deeply and evenly when feeling stressful.

THE POWER OF WORDS

We often approach the day with a particular attitude or feeling. Whether it is negative or positive depends upon our frame of mind. We awaken thinking "I feel good"; then our day develops into a very positive, productive day. Often we awaken feeling negative. Instead of allowing this mood to dictate the day's events, simply try this exercise in positive thinking.

1. Closing eyes, relax the body and begin watching the normal breath flow.
2. Feel your chest rising and falling, expanding and relaxing.
3. As you inhale, simply say to yourself the syllable ham, and as you exhale repeat the syllable sa.
   Continue this process, always keeping your awareness on your breath and the syllables you are repeating.
5. When the mind wanders, simply return to the technique.
6. Do this whenever you're feeling tense or agitated, in order to become more relaxed and balanced.
7. This is a wonderful technique to use for insomnia or when encountering anxiety symptoms.

The simple phrase, *Hamsa*, is a very positive word to use in order to bring about a sense of well being and mental clarity. Classically called a mantra, the word Hamsa means I AM THAT, meaning I am that quietness, that happiness, that feeling of balance and harmony.

MEDITATION

Webster's Dictionary defines meditation as sustained contemplation. What we strive to contemplate is our own sense of well being.

Meditation is:

1. Healthy—blood pressure and hypertension can virtually be eliminated through control of anxiety.
2. Convenient—it can be done anywhere and at any time.
3. Cost effective—it is a tool that each individual can use on his own. It doesn't cost money to simply relax.
4. Good for business—when you're more relaxed and feeling positive, all that you come in contact with will show the effects.
5. Concentration—through mental clarity you are able to focus on results, therefore becoming more effective in attaining your goals.

Meditation can make an incredible and unforgettable difference in your life. Meditative sessions not only leave you feeling great, and wonderfully refreshed, but also through a technique called superlearning can be used to improve business, sports and academics.

In 1966, the Bulgarian Ministry of Education founded the Center for Suggestopedia at the Institute of Suggestology. The staff taught class and conducted physiological and medical research as they observed the development of rapid learning and supermemory. The classes used lounge chairs, subdued lights, and quiet music as the students read materials. The graduates absorbed and remembered 120 to 150 new words from a two-hour session. Many of them emerged fluent in foreign languages.

The preparation for superlearning involves relaxation with affirmations, breathing to a beat, soft music, and materials to recall. Recently, my daughter and I enrolled for a self-hypnosis class using The textbook *Superlearning*, by Sheila Ostrander and Lynn Schroeder. The instructor used tapes with suggestions and baroque music that was recorded under the narrator's voice. Also, my daughter was enrolled in a real estate course at the same time. She recorded her real estate course with baroque music and listened to her tapes 2-3 times each day. She passed her exams on the first try with very high scores.

Meditation, relaxation, superlearning and baroque music have been used to speed healing and to insure recovery after major surgery. The most effective use seemed to occur as people respond to their own voices, pre-recorded tapes purchased with the voice of a stranger can be very helpful. However, best results seem to be attained when hearing our own voices. Perhaps our sub-conscious builds upon a friendly relationship which it has established within us for results.

Joy in learning is a basic tenet underlying superlearning, Superlearning systems aim at the painless birth of knowledge, free of tension and boredom. Learning is a pleasure, not a problem because superlearning uses relaxation and meditation and is stressfree. [100]

All the Cotton Is Picked

CHAPTER SIX

CHAPTER SIX

All the Cotton Is Picked

"In de dead of night I sometimes, git to t'inking of de pas',
An' de days w'en slavery helt me in my mis'ry — ha'd an' fas'"
Dough de time was mighty tryin',
In dese houahs somehow hit seem,
Dat a brightah light come slippin',
Thoo de kivahs of my dream.
        The Old Cabin — Paul Lawrence Dunbar — 1985

This chapter is entitled "All the Cotton Is Picked," because many old tried and true techniqes for use at work are sadly outdated. There has been an evolution from slave labor to the present conditions faced by "Buppies" (Black Upwardly Mobile Professionals) in the workplace.

Co-publishers John and Carolyn Mitchell from Odyssey West Magazine of Denver, gave their permission for me to use reprints of articles published in 1983 and 1984, from my Advice column. Readers, colleagues, seminar participants, and strangers wrote to me and asked for answers to their questions about career development and business opportunities. Based on interviews, research and experience, I responded to the readers' questions found in this chapter. In some cases, I was able to follow up and to know the actual outcomes of the situations. I have reported what happened in those cases where I was privileged to know the final outcomes. Some of the cases ended with a brighter light slipping through the covers of that person's dream.

When all the cotton was finally picked and the farmland in the South had lost its fertility, Black women had to redefine their roles in the workplace. After World War II ended, all the bombs had been exploded and the men returned to their jobs in factories, women washed the TNT dust off their industrial gloves, hung up their welder's shields and redefined their roles in the world of work. Since the Civil Rights Movement appeared to be led by and fought for Black males, Black women made valiant attempts to pursue career goals, utilize affirmative action programs and found their rights undermined and redefined as Women's Rights. Then, the Women's Movement resulted in the right to sleep around, and otherwise imitate the dress and other mannerismn of men in our society. These goals had little or no appeal for Black women. Black females asked repeatedly, "What has the enemy done about the quality of family, work or political life that would make me want to act or be like him?" Again, Black women faced the challenge of the double whammy, racism and sexism, and decided to regroup, reassess, and redefine roles and goals.

After "All the Cotton Was Picked" America began economic, political, and social restructuring and so it is that contemporary minorities and women ponder the question: "What do I do now that 'all the cotton is picked'?" Every corporation has a paper compliance document called an affirmative action plan, every governmental agency has at least a token Black female middle-level manager, every business has one Black superwoman sales representative, every financial insitution has one assistant to the assistant vice president in charge of minority affairs. The questions became how minorities and women are going to accomplish new beginnings and/or how do they operate in the restructuring of America after all the cotton is picked.

The bad news is that "all the cotton is picked." According to M. Scott Peck in his book, *The Road Less Traveled*, "Life is difficult."[101] The good news is that Black women have been here before, have met the challenges, have fought on, have survived the battles, and have prospered as they responded to the burden of the "Silken, Yes, But Strings." Khadijah Farabi-Nance, president of Syadia Creations, discussed the silken strings in her speech entitled "It Doesn't Have To Be A Hobby." Farabi-Nance described the four silken strings that further complicate the restructuring of work and the quality of life for minorities and women as follows:

Silken String # One:	Yes, but are women really prepared, qualified, and capable?
Silken String # Two:	Yes, but does the establishment have enough hard data for assurances that women have the emotional stability for upper level management?
Silken String # Three:	Yes, but are women really serious about work, or is work just a hobby for them?
Silken String # Four:	Yes, but wil she be a strong fighter, full of confidence or will she be a victim?

Yes, but, questions like will she, is she, could she, would she, can be answered with Tools For Survival that provide a workable formula for success. Many workers have perfected Guerrilla Warfare as a tool. Guerrilla warfare involves strategies such as playing high card winners slowly, preparing a graceful, yet sudden disengagement, as well as capitalizing on small victories by parlaying them into large gains. Another tool is to know and to use the published rules, regulations and procedures. Many organizations operate with practices that seriously violate their own procedural manuals. Sometimes just minding your own business could become a tool for survival.

While a positive neutral stance is appropriate and effective for a new employee, professional assertivists are those workers who survive swimming with sharks over the long term. The risks are ever present. Kate Vozoff says, "If you reach out to join the crowd, there's a chance you'll be cruelly rejected. If you speak up for all that you want and believe in, you bait the demoralization that accompanies a refusal. If you do your job exceedingly well, there's the strong possibility that some will respond with jealously level resentment." Women must struggle to seek the balance of their efforts so that even critics must report that women are excellent in their chosen fields of endeavor.

In order to analyze and to adopt a meaningful, useful and practical formula for the successful pursuit of survival, what would be found as essential ingredients in a Tools for Survival formula? The formula would include one part gypsy, who is flexible and ready to move, who is eager to try new things, and probably most important, one who lives by this philosophy behind the Romain Gary quote:

> Humor is an affirmation of dignity,
> A declaration of man's superiority
> to all that befalls him.

Next, add one part psychic. This portion of the formula requires that persons with a sixth sense use it and those without the sixth sense develop and sharpen it. The test is to develop a pattern of movement that leads you to get a "break" when you need one. Finally, the formula for successful pursuit of survival must have one part mystery. Without implying dishonesty, the one part mystery means that things are planned and implemented in secret. That secrecy simply neutralizes adversarial positioning. When mystery surrounds certain aspects of the life of a woman, she may appear to be one who is likely to do audacious, spontaneous things. A mysterious Black woman would be doggedly stubborn about R.O.I. (return on investment), and R.F.E. (reward for effort). Rather than being stigmatized because of her position, she'd be labelled a mysterious person with ability, determination, and perseverance. Pour one part Gypsy, one part psychic, and one part mystery over chunks of intelligence, blend with a large measure of self-assessment, add a dash of grit and serve "One-Day-At-A-Time."

Paying Dues, Singing the Blues

Dear Martha,

I have been given 30 days notice of termination on my present job. I have not been a successful candidate either at passing tests for or getting through the interview for other positions. I am 30 years old, a Black female, and I have a master's degree. However, my jobs usually last from six (6) months to one and one-half (1½) years, but, no longer. Since this has been going on since I left college, the pattern has begun to bother me, my parents, and my friends. When I discuss my dilemma, everyone talks about being willing to "pay your dues." I don't want to work on the same job for 30 years and retire like my folks did. Is that what these people are talking about? Is this message about "dues paying" something to which I should or must give attention?

H.A.H. - Denver

Dear H.A.H.:

Since the 1950's, Americans have spent time identifying our "piece of the rock," fixing some more "instant" pudding or polishing some more glossy plastic. Our failure was in thinking that the "rock," the "pudding," and the "plastic" were the solution rather than the sweat, prayers, and toil of the people, both males and females, educated and illiterate, Blacks and Caucasians. Blacks suffer the conflict between understanding the mixed messages about what their rights are and what their privileges are in the world of work.

I consider the Black woman who cleans and washes for me a professional person. She paid her dues while working for Caucasians in the South for many years. That paid account allows her to state now, "I'll never clean for anyone except my own folk."

My generation was taught to respect our elders just because they were older. I believe that to be Black and to grow old in America is proof of victories over situations that neither you nor I could comprehend. One implication in the slang greeting "Hello Home" between Blacks was that the person greeting you knew you, and the old folks back at "home." This person might be able to tell you something to help you based on a trip down wisdom alley with the old Black sage or griot from "home."

Don't let a false sense of security or a plastic sophistication make you close your ears to an important message about the blues and the dues of Black folks. Remember Blacks, like your parents, who worked 30 years on the job, who lived to retire, and who lived to tell about it, are living monuments to two important truths. First, years ago, most Blacks were not employed on any kind of job where one could remain and retire after 30 years, excluding teachers and Pullman porters. So give respect to the prayer and determination that your parents and mine had in order to accomplish a goal of such magnitude. Just think of the endurance and faith that they demonstrated daily in order to meet the formidable obstacles in the workplace. Secondly, recall that the Civil Rights Act of 1965 was passed during your short lifetime. So paying dues for Blacks has meant vigilance without support, resilience without reward, and perseverance without reinforcement. Ultimately, you will pay your dues knowing that you must start 30 yards behind others in the starting blocks.

With a lot of help from the Great Spirit, parents, and friends, you will manage to stay in the race and to pay your dues. Attend to the message that you are being given. Start out by dedicating a humble ear that listens, and a young heart that is open to respect the message and the giver.

Dear Martha:

I resented and resisted your response to my question. But, I'm writing this letter to tell you that your column nagged at me.

My job did terminate. I was forced to go home and to go through the application, interview, selection process. I am now gainfully employed in a job that I love and plan to stay on for as long as possible.

I made two startling discoveries after beginning to look inside for answers. First, I had not had a fulfilling personal life. My dreams were on hold. Secondly, the discontent about my personal life made me deaf, dumb, and blind to positive suggestions from family and friends. The discontent caused me to constantly sing the blues.

Somehow, being out of a job that I hated drew more positive people to me. My positive mental attitude improved, followed by my interactions with others. My marriage and family life followed closely.

Well, thanks to some gentle nudging from you, "I've come a long way, baby!!"

Your article about paying dues surprised me. I would have expected you to say things like "do your thing," or "times have changed." You just plain blew me away with the notion that "paying dues for Black folks meant vigilance without support, resilience without reward, and perseverance without reinforcement."

I looked at those words and realized that I use them in my formula for saving money and acquiring what I want for my home, my husband, and my yard. Why not, then, for my career?

Since your advice, I've had a baby, returned to work, and plan to settle into a pattern of dues paying for job success.

H.A.H. — Denver

Becoming an Entrepreneur

Dear Martha:

I am a 42-year-old Black female. My daughter is on her own, 22-years-old, and has a four-year-old daughter. I live with a very special and supportive person. I have had a successful career in a highly competitive sales, marketing and public relations field, My annual salary is well over $40,000. My dream has always been to operate my own business. How can I be sure of which business, when I am ready to go out on my own, and whether or not I could become a successful entrepreneur?

G.P. — Aurora

Dear G.P.:

The make-up of your question gives me some tips about your approach to problem-solving. You looked at your broad universe and then honed in on a few action lines. Such an approach would be very helpful to any entrepreneur. You see, I perceive you as a person on the move, that is, ready to move over, move out, move in, move up, or move by whatever means you determine to be your targets or goals.

Albert Shapero in *SAVVY* reported finding in a poll taken in the U.S.A., as many as 70 to 80 percent of the population would like to become entrepreneurs. However, relatively few of those persons translate their wishes into their real lives. Shapero also found that those people who do start their own businesses seem to follow a common pattern that includes four major factors: 1) displacement, 2) a propensity to take control of one's life, 3) the perception that it is feasible to operate a business and 4) resources.

"Scratch an entrepreneur and most likely you'll find a displaced person," says Shapero. Your letter indicates that the fast pace and related stress in your "highly competitive" job have become a health hazard. Further, you state that a portion of your 40K is spent nursing your blood pressure to keep it down. You describe typical stress factors which medical literature has documented as especially applicable to Black people in America. Voila! Displacement!

Your selection of the kind of business that you should plan to open should be based on some quiet time spent responding to questions about self assessment. The importance of self assessment cannot be overemphasized. You might start with questions such as: 1) What do I like and dislike? 2) What are some things that create irreconcilable differences? 3) What skills do I use to perform tasks well consistently? 4) What am I doing when I feel as if I've hit the "sweet spot" in my racket?

#31   TOOL FOR SURVIVAL

Self-assessment is a tool which gives birth to the unborn self-concept.

Knowing and confirming one's career and human worth can reduce the adverse effects of job changes such as being denied salary increases and promotions, firing, and layoff.

Self assessment should be done using questions from two other categories, namely, 1) self assessment of human worth, and 2) self assessment of career worth. You might enjoy taking the Career Quest Test and answering the list of questions that you will find in the book *Tools for Survival* on page 84. When the answers to human and career worth questions are added to information about prestige, title, and salary, you will find glistening clues to the bank of skills which you possess.

You may be surprised to know how many things you can do well consistently. If your skills bank is quite filled, you are probably ready to examine those skills. You will find the answer to the nature of, the scope of, and the content of the business which you could operate on your own. Your level of readiness for a people persuasion business seems quite high at this time. You certainly must have presented yourself well to have been successful in your current career in sales and marketing. You are not a mono-dimensional person since you have built a career in public relations, a highly competitive field. Also, your career involvement has provided you with some knowledge of the duties of a CEO, a treasurer, and a secretary. Based on skills identification, self assessment, interests, needs and your tolerance for change, you are ready to select your most compatible area in which to do business.

George Trower-Subira says in his book *Black Folks' Guide to Making Big Money in America* that the answer to when you should start your own business is found in the existence of two conditions. First, you should have identified a market for your product and secondly, you should have found the resources to cover necessary expenses. Necessary expenses are defined as those expenses that get you and your product to your public or audience. Remember that 98 percent of all businesses are small. Even the most successful of small businesses often were started 50 years ago in a one room apartment or in the present owner's basement. The office space, the staff, and the beautiful art pieces that you see now came after the tons of hard work and long hours with little or no glamour. One of the Tools in my book says "It takes a lot of slow to grow! It's hard by the yard, but a cinch by the inch!"

The last part of your question asks how you can be sure that you will be a successful entrepreneur. You have the key ingredient in my opinion, that is, you have always known that you wanted to work for yourself. My view is shared by Rollene Saal, former editor of Bantam Books. Saal says that the steps that take people over the big hurdles in business are made by people who know what they want, who accept risks, who trust their feelings, who maintain professional contacts, who do their homework, and people who are decisive. In *Tools*, I say that you should not feel compelled to explain yourself away to everyone who asks. Many people who ask questions such as "How are you going to make it?" could never understand any answer that you might attempt. You will need your energy for pursuits where there is some return on your investment. I heard one author say that "a book talked about, is a book never written!"

The success of any entrepreneur depends upon their ability to diversify and to intensify their efforts. Black women have a long history of working for pay inside and outside the home. Therefore, Black women have demonstrated the capability to do more than one thing at a time. Diversification as a hedge against failure for the entrepreneur means using such abilities and doing several things at the same time to increase one's earning power. For example, a flight attendant may also do consulting as a fashion coordinator. If you decide to open your own business, you could earn money as a consultant in your present career in sales and marketing.

#59   TOOL FOR SURVIVAL

DIVERSIFY!

You really can do more than one thing in a lifetime.

Divert your talents and skills into many areas in order to increase your earning power and to enhance your personal power.

Biographies of successful business people indicate that they all worked 80-100 hours per week. Part of that work was a resource called "sweat equity" but the other portion was an attempt to have something going strong in case the other part of the business hit a slump. Plan to diversify and to use your "sweat equity."

You are very wise to give accolade to your special supportive person (man). Human beings need a sense of belonging for their well being. The toughness in the world of work makes us need a sincere, supportive, reinforcing system of stroking and reward, completely separate from the work arena. Take time to appreciate the man in your personal life. Remember that a Mercedes Benz is not the only symbol of the good life. Tell your man often the words used by the golfer Lee Trevino, "I can feel it when I drive." You are fortunate to have each other. Continue to care for, to nourish, and to renew that relationship.

Dear Martha,

Thank you for giving me such a comprehensive answer to my question. I thought you might like to know how I used your advice.

First, I used your 4 question test for self-assessment. I took several days to just answer four questions. The answers kept changing. Then I realized that I could only think like I was supposed to answer on the first round. During round two, I asked "What would I like if I could have my heart's desire?" The answers were then totally different.

My skills bank was filled with useful but seldom used skills. You often hear how helpful people found writing things down. Well, it does truly make a difference. I started with the list that you gave me in the article. Somehow, I had never recognized all of my hard work and the lessons learned that were paid for with long hours, sweat, and tears.

I want to send you a special thanks for speaking positively, with encouraging comments about Black women. I needed that ego booster. All of this media hype and social science literature about "disadvantaged" and "minorities" has created an energy drain for me that I needed to shut off.

Also, I'm reading again. I started with Maya Angelou's auto-biographies. I could feel the birth of my unborn self-concept.

Look out world. "I can feel it when I drive."

G.P. — Aurora

Give In or Give Up: Discouraged

Dear Martha:

I own a secretarial, mail-drop and answering service. I have equipment that was first installed in expensive office space where my business prospered for one and one-half years. The business slowdown that hit everyone caused my customers to stop taking new services and to stop paying me. Finally, I had to choose between paying for the office and paying my $350 per month home mortgage. I moved my business into my home. Business is very slow, but I managed to pay one-half of the new installment cost for the second installation of the equipment. I am tied to the phone deck all day because I can't afford to pay for a helper. A helper that I could train to handle the phones while I went out would allow me to market my business. My problem is further complicated by the fact that the phone company cuts off my service for 2-3 days each week. I need a six month extension to pay the bill that I owe so that I can get new customers. I wish that they would give me this consideration since I have paid over $7000 to the company over the past two years.

However, when new clients inquire about service, I cannot aggres-
sively pursue contracts with them because I am afraid that my
phones will be cut off without warning. One week, I was granted a
10-day extension and then two days later I had no service. If I could
borrow $5000, I could keep going. I am so tired and discouraged. I
am a Black, female, single parent with five dependent children. I
don't know what I would do if SBA exercised the lien that they hold
on my home for the loan that they granted me to get started. Maybe I
should just give up and look for a job. What do you think?

J.D. — Denver

Dear J.D.:

Your problem has been written about in business management literature under the heading of why small business owners fail. Through no fault of your own, you do not have enough owner's equity to invest in your success nor do you have any access to reserve capital. Many women who own businesses use the resources of the family, whether children or a husband, when they have to weather an economic slump such as the one you described. Without reserve capital, you will experience more and more frustration. Another way of saying this is to state that it takes money to make money.

You are also trying to sell a service. Traditionally, service industries are harder to build, to market, and to make successful even during lucrative monetary periods. Products can be packaged and taken to a financial institution where someone will be able to understand what you do based on what they see. Because you provide a service, when you approach a banker, you have little to show and it is even harder to describe your target market.

You could develop a business plan that shows how many customers you would need for how long in order to get back into the black. But, without being able to leave the phones to enthusiastically market your service with dependable help that would keep your present customers happy, you are in a huge ocean with a very small boat. Borrowing any more would place your home in jeopardy. You should definitely not put your property or your credit rating at any further risk.

Embark on a three part plan: first, look for a job where you can earn the best possible salary for your skills; secondly, pay something to any creditor that has an interest in your property; and thirdly, continue to try to pay on the equipment that you have from the phone company. In the future when you have satisfied your obligations and have healed a bit from the frustration and anguish of this experience, you may be able to put together enough reserve capital to try small business ownership again. Your children will be older, and you will have taken some time to breathe and re-evaluate your goals. In your job search, start with some of your customers who may have companies where they would love to have you as a regular full-time employee. Remember that you don't have to sell yourself to them because they already know you and the quality of your work. Stay close to your spiritual self and know that I am sending you strength waves. Add prayer, meditation, good food, good rest, and positive friends to the tips above and you can't miss being successful.

Dear Martha,

Because I had adopted the philosophy that says, "A quitter never wins and a winner never quits," I needed your Advice Column to give me permission to step back.

Subsequent to your article in Odyssey West Magazine, in phone conversation you encouraged me to take my first vacation in five years. I can't believe I did that, but I did. I went to California and sat by a swimming pool for a week. What a difference that week has made in my life! I had no idea how really tired and totally weakened I had become.

I stayed in California for a month. Everyday that I was away brought me a rush of healing. I've returned to a weight loss program and a long-term assignment with a temporary service. I've enrolled in school and plan to complete my college degree. I plan to take a full-time job as soon as I feel better.

This may sound like a lot, but everything seems so much more manageable since I'm not feeling like a failure. I've paid small amounts on all my bills and my creditors have been cooperative.

Thank you for the tip about "good food, meditation, and good rest," I gave in but I didn't give up on me.

J.D. — Denver

Forced Off the Career Track

Dear Martha,
    Three years ago, I was advised to accept a transfer and a promotion with a move to Denver in order to gain upward mobility with my company. I agreed to and did both based on discussions with the corporate recruiter. She informed me that three of the company's vice presidents had once held the job which I was being offered. Further, she assured me that this transfer and promotion definitely would put me on the career track which provided the talent pool for the upwardly mobile males in the company. Presently, my salary is over $30K. I am able to increase my earning power because I have a profitable avocation. My hobby has brought me so much joy that it is my true career goal. However, I feel betrayed and I am confused and very angry about what has happened on my job. Three Caucasian males who were all hired after I was, in the same position, have moved right by me. They have all been promoted and I was not even interviewed for the positions. Is this racism at work? Was it my mistake to move to a new city and to take this promotion? I had high hopes that a Black male could pursue the same career path that had proved successful for others in the company.

R.S. — Montbello

Dear R.S.:
    I'd like you to know that recently I have received eight similar inquiries. So, this issue of unfulfilled promises is facing many people in the workforce. In some of the literature, this new wave of crushing disappointments is called playing hard ball in the world of work. Fernandez found in studying the views of managers' awareness of the complications faced by minorities' corporate work life that data obtained from Caucasians showed that Caucasian males have more difficulty than other groups in seeing problems with their system. These males do not perceive any degree of unfairness with the way their system responds to obstacles that impede the progress and movement through the hierarchy for Black men and other minorities (*Racism and Sexism in Corporate Life*, 1981, Lexington).
    You have made the sacrifice to move and the adjustments to function in a new location. Your letter points out that you are

networking to promote your hobby which has become your major career goal. You are happy with your business and your social contacts. So, chin up, chest out, and smiles all around are in order. You have not made a mistake at all. You are right where you need to be to become a fortune builder. George Trower-Subira says in his book *Black Folks Guide to Making Big Money in America* that one of the characteristics of fortune builders is their ability to do more than one thing consistently well. Your salary, plus the creative budgeting technique of using your hobby to increase your income may not make you upwardly mobile by Caucasian male standards, but since you are a young, gifted and Black male, you are on track to enjoy and to build a fortune using the norms and standards that have been tried and proven true for Booker T., Carver, Bethune, and Maya. Kanter found when examining large companies such as yours that minorities and women were perceived as and were treated as tokens. Goodmeasure, Inc., described these tokens as persons who have no or very low access to actual power, opportunity and proportional influence and/or strategies in the workplace. However, when Kanter found women and minorities who had been fortunate enough to increase their levels of power, opportunity and proportion in an organization, she described them as effective leaders and persons who exercised their authority in productive ways. Kanter found the most collaborative, humane environments for women to be retailing. My observations for Black males is that small business owners and entrepreneurs had more opportunities, had system power, and exhibited an interest in empowering subordinates. In such an environment, workers could be known as "comers,"; as everyone would be in a more favorable position in the power structure and race and sex differences would play a much more limited role in their upward mobility.

In a recent discussion about what to use as a conference theme, we considered the topic "Up Your Ladder." You have arrived up your ladder. My only caution is one made by Adele Scheele in her book *Skills for Success*. Scheele categorizes all people into the two groups sustainers and achievers. Sustainers are workers who spend 70% of their time working hard and 30% of their time waiting for praise, recognition, grades, and feedback from others such as teachers, bosses or supervisors. Sustainers need reassurance that their 70% was appreciated and was recognized. The deadly trap for sustainers is that when the recognition, reward, or reinforcement does not come back to the degree felt compatible with the 70% output, sustainers begin to lament. Lamentations lead to complaints, complaints lead to resentment, resentment to non-productivity, non-productivity to unacceptable levels of stress, high level of stress to agitation and irritation, and on to chronic conditions such as alcoholism and drug abuse.

Racism and sexism are both here to stay because they are profitable and useful strategies in the workplace. However, minorities and women are also here to stay. Fernandez calls what you face neo-racism. It is the more subtle and sophisticated form of racism. Neo-racism is the insidious combination of traditional institutional racism with covert, quiet, exclusionary behaviors built into the very fiber of organizations. Your letter told me that your yearly performance review rated you as an outstanding employee. So no one has identified any skill deficit that would set you apart from the males who were promoted.

You are a fortune builder and an achiever. Carefully write down some goals for your avocation. Enjoy your job, be thankful for your salary and invest some of it into your new ideas and your future as an entrepreneur. You may find some ideas in my book *TOOLS* that will help you to elevate your thoughts to the benefits of personal power, new ideas, new ways for marketing your varied skills, and new contacts for adventure and achievement. Upward mobility means making your dream a reality. As an achiever you are resourceful and should continue to keep on keeping on!

Getting There:
The Costs of Starting Your Business

Dear Martha,
When will I know that I've invested enough of my own money in my business. My friends tell me that I shouldn't continue with these twelve hour days. I would like to do a new business plan and design an operating plan forecast with a new company brochure. How will I know if my business is a success?

W.T.C. — Denver

Dear W.T.C.

Your letter made me wish that I could refer you to a weekly meeting called "Entrepreneurs Support Group." Since I don't know one, I'll try to discuss your questions as if we were sitting down talking about these things.

First of all, the lack of movement of your business that you feel is a fairly common malady for minority business enterprise owners. The inability to make decisions and to act on those decisions is based partially on the fact that small business ownership is an enterprise that requires work alone for long hours. Further, your commitment and determination may be misunderstood, misjudged, and may even be reduced to the level of ridiculous exchanges. You can observe in our community that small business ownership has very low social status. By comparison, those who work for corporations and organizations enjoy a much greater degree of recognition for their efforts.

Let me share from a speech I've found helpful. This quote has built into it a large measure of gentle nudging as well as a bit of quiet faith. Oliver Wendell Holmes, Jr., in an 1897 Brown University commencement address said:

"In the first stage one has companions, cold and black though it may be, and if he sticks to it, he finds at last that there is a drift as was foretold. When he has found that he has learned the first part of his lesson, that one is safe in trusting to courage and to time."

So do not despair. Pursue each day quietly and peacefully, yet with enthusiasm and vigor. The winners are among those who "finish of the race." It is the "finish of the race" that makes one an "overcomer." Take care of your views, shield your work energies from negative blows, and by all means rise up from each defeat, brushing off that dust in order to move forward once again. As Susan L. Taylor, editor of *Essence Magazine*, says, "No matter what the adversity, I've always been victorious when I've trusted love to be my guide. The only time it doesn't work is when we forget to use it."

Now for the easy part of your question. Yes, you need an operating plan forecast that includes an organization chart, and your business plan put into dollars and predictions about dollars. Your business plan should show your dollar volume of business that you could expect over the next 12 months. Your plan will account for start-up costs and all expenses. Any size business operation will cost to provide the service. The amount of money left over after the end of the year is your profit. Profit is important because that is your pay.

A management consultant could help you with the design of your company brochure. You may also need a company capability statement that could accompany your brochure. The same business and management consultant could assist you to set up a record keeping system, could prepare a loan package and/or financial information for your firm. By securing the expert professional services of a management consultant, you could be assured that you'd be presented to financial institutions in the most positive, correct, and appropriate fashion. Money spent for such a service is a good investment if you select one who has represented clients like yourself who successfully gained a line of credit or a loan.

Once you work with a competent management consultant, and they learn your business, they can help you to market your product or services. Your consultant could act as an agent who would develop, write and present proposals for you. According to Sandy Bankhead at Travel/Travel, University Hills, after one year in business, she is ready to engage a management consultant. Sandy states that as proprietor she needs to continue the personal attention that she has always given to old customers. She sees her consultant as an extension of the services that she provides. That is, the management consultant develops and presents bids and proposals for new clients and works on ideas that attract new customers for Travel/Travel. This plan is one that would require some immediate cash outlay. However, you should be able to see an immediate return on your investment in the form of new customers, new markets, a larger line of credit, and successfully bid contracts.

In the last part of your letter you asked when you could stop putting more of your capital into the business. The answer depends on your situation and how you answer the following questions. Do you need to expand sales and services in order to remain in business? Do you have more money to put into the business? Would you borrow from friends and relatives? Could you borrow from the bank? Would your suppliers arrange liberal credit terms? Do you need the loan for equipment, fixtures, employees' salaries, or other expenses? When can you expect a return on your investment? If you must have this money to put into action your operating plan forecast, then, by all means, go for it! Stay alert to changing conditions in your company and adjust your business plan accordingly.

After you examine both the technological and the marketing changes, you must determine a time for completing the revisions needed in your plan. Perhaps you could use a felt marker to make a sign in bold letters with the following quote from the Holmes 1897 Brown University commencement address that says:

"But he has not yet learned all. All for his trials have been those of his companions. But if he is a man of high ambitions, he must leave even his fellow — adventures and go forth into a deeper solitude and greater trials. He must start for the pole. In plain words, he must face the loneliness of original work. No one can cut new paths in company. He does that alone."

New Job: To Be or Not To Be

Dear Martha,

I am a male who has taught elementary school for four years. Teachers are required to hold a master's degree in order to remain in teaching. I decided to take some computer courses. However, my employment history shows experience in jobs related only to education. Are my prospects good for finding a job in the computer field?

L.B. — Denver

Dear L.B.:

The skills which you have developed while working in the field of education are highly transferrable in the world of work. Your training included the development of planning, organization, and evaulation skills. These skills are found in every type of business and industry. Most especially will your problem solving skills enhance your computer capabilities.

John Bensink asserts in *Money Magazine* that employers prefer adults who have earned their knowledge on the job and have lots of direct hands-on experience. As a teacher, you must demonstrate knowledge of subject matter as you help others to learn. Your teacher/learner skills are probably well developed and will be valuable to you as you explore the information about computers.

In your letter, you mention some negative comments from persons who work on large main frame computers. There is a trend which leads some technology-oriented people to think that they are in an elite group which makes them say things such as, 'oh, you're just a teacher', or 'you do not have adequate math preparation.' Seek positive relationships with people who work with computers. I suggest that you contact organizations and people who work with microcomputers. Find approachable people who will share their experiences with you. Ask them to tell you about members of their network. Accept luncheon invitations and go to listen and to learn all that you can.

You might consider accepting a secretarial position as one method of entering the computer field. The old traditional secretary and the traditional office as we have known them in the past are fast becoming obsolete. Today, almost all offices use some form of computer. You could gain needed practice while you begin to develop some variety in your resume. As a secretary, you could also take advantage of any workshop seminar, or training programs that are offered by your employer. Remember to be a sponge. You can learn a great deal from others.

Do some research on job descriptions for positions in the computer field. Begin to seek experiences that match some of those descriptions. For example, data base operators, computer sales, and computer repair are three very different jobs. You may have a friend or a relative who owns a television or small appliance repair shop. If you were interested in computer repair, you could go there to learn the use of hand tools.

Look for small firms which need pleasant, willing workers. Use your summer vacation to take advantage of a change in your regular occupation. Read, read, read, and keep your eyes and ears open. Let people in the computer field know that you are considering a change of career.

Dear Martha,
I am a single parent with a 14-month-old daughter, a full time job and I'm enrolled in college courses. If I didn't have to work, I could go to school as a full-time student. I am willing to tough it out on welfare and student loans if I have to do that. Should I quit my job and devote more of my time to completing my degree?
S.B. — Aurora

Dear S.B.:

We live in a very conservative era with money constraints and an economic slump which is quite real. However, women in the world of work *are* the norm rather than the exception. Many women find that the special skills needed to balance dual careers, that is, job and school, are extremely challenging and time consuming. Further, you have the complicated challenge of single parenting and the care of a very young child.

The conditions that you face all present troublesome concerns that will require non-traditional solutions. That should not frighten you, but you must make note so that you are certain to seek non-traditional solutions to non-traditional problems. For example, students are no longer eligible for welfare payments if they are full time students.

Only a few years ago, I could have advised you to quit your job and to commit more of your energies to school. During the 80's, I would suggest that you will need a substantial employment history in order to find a suitable position. I do not advise you to hang on to your job out of fear, but rather to hang on to your job because you have a much needed tool that assures your economic independence.

Student loans and welfare result in Pay Now and Pay Later. On the other hand, if you pay your dues now with all three of your major activities balanced, you will only pay now, but will reap the benefits later.

Contacts can mean contracts. There is no guarantee that you will meet a potential employer at the college. However, you may hear about or meet people in your field if you are out in the world of work.

Back to Basics for Job Success

Dear Martha,

I have worked two years for a large financial institution. As a result of my business school coursework and on-the-job training, my skills are excellent. I speak well and am able to compose standard business responses, use all office machines, and I type 80 w.p.m. My problem surfaced last week when I was denied promotion and/or transfer by two departments because my work record showed that I had been reprimanded several times for arriving late to work. I am a young mother with a selfish and demanding husband. He often becomes hostile just before we go to work. Sometimes he just refuses to drive the car until we finish our argument. No matter what I do, or how I plan, his tirades upset me, our three-year-old son, and my daily schedule. How can I deal with this problem so that I am on time for work? Can I be promoted at this company?

J.A.H. — Denver

Dear J.A.H.:

Let's look at answers to your questions based on a statement of the problem, an examination of the not-so-obvious factors, and solutions. Yes, you can be promoted at that same company, but you must take some immediate actions on both the home-front and in the workplace.

Being late is described in social science volumes as a problem that seems to plague minority workers. The stereotype for lazy and late has been assigned to minorities for ages. I agree with Grier and Cobbs who wrote in *Black Rage*, "We take the position that there is a grain of truth in every stereotypical canard tossed at the brothers. But we move a step further. A close examination of the trait, its psychological roots, and its predictable transformations may yield interesting conclusions. Oppression, which is capable of producing paralyzing fear and paranoia, may under slightly different circumstances produce the deadliest of enemies."

Fear is one of the deadliest enemies to human beings. Many people are late arriving at jobs where they do not value the goals of the organization. Others are late to jobs where they have hostility about the nature of the job or they fear the amount of responsibility or lack of accountability experienced. Still other workers, and I see you in this group, are late to their jobs because they accept and are burdened with too many roles and assignments that must be accomplished before they ever get to work. If you had asked me to tell you what your problem was, I would have said, "You try to take care of too many things, too much of the time, in too short a period, that is, on a daily basis." I would wager that your daily tasks would rival others weekly list of things to do.

Have you considered the thought that you probably do not have adequate transportation for a two pay-check family when a single tantrum can immobilize the entire family? You have not been given a choice here. You must join a car pool, pay for a ride to work, or use public transportation. The family's reaction to an independent move like this may be a pleasant surprise to you.

The solutions to your problem are not simple, but they do require that you go back to the basics. Do you have an alarm clock in a place where your husband cannot shut it off before you hear it? Do you need another course in computers to round out your educational background? Should you make the sacrifice to have a second car? Do you need to remain in your present job until you feel stronger and more confident about your family life? Would you really be at your best if you had to learn a new set of people and office politics? Do you ignore the hazards to mind and body from prolonged stress caused by unresolved conflict?

Perhaps you should give yourself a rest by remaining in this same department since the reprimands have not threatened your position.

Now, how can you be on time for work? Tonight, when you prepare for bed, determine that you will not be late again. Then step-by-step, take positive-aggressive, assertive steps to assure that your morning moves, no matter how hard, from bed to work. Your schedule must be one that you determine is adequate, appropriate, and practical. A basic understanding about work is that your job performance should be good after you arrive at work. But your record will not assess your performance if you do not arrive on time. You need to be viewed as trustworthy and dependable if you are to improve your pay. People who are not punctual receive very negative performance ratings.

Just another hunch about a part of your fear about taking charge of your pattern of movement. Are you afraid that you may not be considered feminine enough by your man if you insist on freedom of movement for the purpose of career empowerment? Collette Dowling, in her book *The Cinderella Complex*, says, "There is a new crisis in femininity, a conflict over what is and what is not feminine, preventing a lot of women from functioning in a happy, well integrated way . . . Women succumbing to what I call 'Gender Panic,' fear that independent behavior is nonfeminine." In order to get promoted at your company, you need to do three things that would be professionally assertive. First, you should have a discussion with your supervisor in which you share the fact that you have identified the root of the problem with punctuality. Tell the supervisor that you would like to enter into a written contract which states that for ninety (90) days, you will be on time every day with no exceptions. That contract should include an agreement to have the supervisor prepare a written review of performance at the end of the three month period. Secondly, you should request that references to your poor attendance be removed after a six month review. The supervisor will probably respond, "Oh, well, I don't know about that," to your request. That's OK, because the jury is really out until you have given them hard evidence of your determination. This is a negotiating point which simply underscores your serious intent. Now you're ready. Your goals and objectives are clear and concise. You know what time it is. Now, as the commercial says, "It's your time!" Check your strategy for the basics — a watch, a clock, a bus schedule, a friend for back-up, a commitment to move, a deaf ear to objections. When you deposit your first check from your salary increase, you'll owe it all to your independent nature, some tools for survival, dogged determination, vigilance, and perseverance.

Reorganization or Termination

Dear Martha,
My supervisor announced the implementation of a reorganization plan in my governmental agency. The result of this new management plan is that all 15 employees have been terminated after being given 30 days notice. Further, our notice tells us that we may apply for and compete for our jobs if vacancies are announced. I have been a loyal employee for three years. My job performance was rated above satisfactory until recently. Last month, I was falsely accused of poor attendance and mismanagement of a budget item. At the time I thought these accusations were innocent mistakes because they were done by a supervisor who had only been on the job for 30 days. Now I don't know where this guy is coming from. What should I do to regain my job and the trust of the program director?
R.R. — Lakewood

Dear R.R.:

Your director approved the staff reorganization plan. She knows and understands the actions of your supervisor that have placed your job at risk. I doubt that the director feels that your trust or the lack of such a relationship with you is important. I hope that this statement does not shock you or affect you as a harsh reality. However, it is obvious to me that you have reached some unrealistic conclusions about your relationshiop with both the director and your new supervisor.

Look at how your situation illumines when you add the following data. First, your director hired the new supervisor. Secondly, the director is the supervisor's boss and must approve any and all components in a reorganization plan. Lastly, you have almost no job protection with a year to year contract having a 30 day notice of termination clause. Also you serve at the pleasure of the supervisor who can renew or not renew your contract.

I made an inquiry to a labor attorney and discovered that the facts in your letter are not one bit unusual. He said that this practice of reorganization is widely used by governmental bureaucracies. Whenever a decision is made to oust someone, the standard practice includes announcing a reorganization plan and terminating all employees.

You may have an internal grievance procedure under which you might bring allegations related to discrimination, breach of contract and/or violations of personnel policies. My guess is that your director and supervisor have adhered to the 30 day notice as set forth in your contract. Also since your employees have been treated alike, your employer's action would be considered fair treatment and without disparate impact.

Get a copy of my book, *Tools For Survival*. Read and use the information in the section "Getting Fired the Right Way." Now is the hour to take time to talk to yourself about new career directions. This change in your life could be a most positive influence. Change that seems to come unexpectedly and appears to be so negative can be a most positive stimulus for you. Your energies should be used to find an employer who needs and appreciates your loyalty and hard work. Though the process of change is painful, the new awareness and wisdom that grow out of change are essential Tools for Survival.

Dear Martha:

My letter should have been signed from "pushing boulders uphill." I've decided not to dedicate the rest of my life to accommodating the stress of career development in a governmental agency.

I was shocked when I talked to people who had been around for years. Most of them hate their supervisors and their jobs. There is a constant struggle going on to get rid of someone. Yet, the Agency itself seems immune to change. The human resource called worker appears to always be in a club of persons called untouchables. Contrary to what you might expect from my use of the word these people are in a club of untouchables who are easily and promptly promoted to the next level when they goof.

My supervisor publicly embarrassed a high-level government official. She was removed by promotion to a new job.

I resigned when the new director tried to implement a similar reorganization. I am now the proud owner of my own firm. Also, I don't think I'd ever have done this if I'd not been displaced and discontent.

Thanks for putting the spotlight on my problems so that I could find my way out of the dark.

Change is truly something that workers need to examine with some new guidelines. This change has been good for me and has been good to me.

W.E.L. — Denver

Myths and Magic of the MBA

Dear Martha,

I am writing this letter because I feel so frustrated. However, I feel guilty about writing because by ordinary standards, I have it made. I am a Black female engineer making a super salary working for a major corporation. My problem is that my course work for my MBA and my job have absorbed my entire life. I have no time for family, friends or to pursue other interests in clubs, organizations and hobbies. I am trying to lead an independent lifestyle. How can I plan my time, manage my career and human goals and avoid social isolation?

W.C.A. — Littleton

Social isolation is a problem experienced often among your peers in corporate life. You grew up, went through school, and then to work, all at a young age. Your goal-directed behavior paid off with the rewards that your career promised. However, you have discovered that some of your social needs cannot be met by job, education, or even a high salary.

My advice is to develop a written plan for the remainder of the year called "My Calendar for Social Networking." On this calendar, list each month with just one activity that you will plan, initiate and conduct. Plan to include the three groups of people with whom you seek to connect. Plan to mix-and-match people whenever possible and practical. For example, plan a small dinner party and invite a classmate, and one of your friends from the job. Keep in mind that you want to reach out to people that you enjoy. You are seeking to stay in contact with people that you care about. I caution you not to invite anyone because of any notion such as "I really ought to." Think carefully about the concepts of having fun and being around enjoyable company. The description of your job success tells me that you have been attending your fair share of the obligatory company functions.

Social networking is different from other social functions because it is carefully planned with your selfish goals as the largest measure of importance. Even family members should be invited only if you sincerely want to be with them. Your personal and professional assertiveness quotient goes up several points each time you are able to decide and to act on your likes and dislikes —and not the horrible "ought to's" sparked by guilt.

I remember the same problem faced me when I sought my doctoral studies. I moved to a predominantly Caucasian town, went to class with new people, and formed new friendships. Though I felt frustrated by the time constraints placed on me by my schedule of studies, I was determined to enjoy this time in my life and to complete my program. When I graduated, I found that some of my old friendships were still intact. Some were even more satisfying than before. I found friendships to be more durable than I had guessed, more dependable than I had hoped, and to need the growth that came with change even more than I had imagined. Those friendships that did not remain were a valuable part of the same growth and change process. Neither partner harbors any regrets.

Rosabeth Moss Kanter, author of *The Change Masters*, says that your generation will have to analyze and to deal with your new role as that of a "corporate entrepreneur." She advises that our new role calls for marketing skills: determining client needs, identifying pressing issues and knowing how ones own skills, abilities and expertise can address those needs. Notice, you determine, you identify, and you decide. Kanter wrote in a 1983 article in *Working Woman* called "Influence Skills" that "standing still means losing ground." So, go ahead with your career and your personal goals for creating social connective tissue. Those who are moving, changing, and growing will be there with you when you complete your studies. The organizations and clubs will be happy to have your membership at a later time.

Dottie Lamm in her *Denver Post* article called "On Planning," examined the question that you asked about planning your life. I agree with Dottie's idea that "planning or not planning can be more than a dilemma. Either can become a trap." Lamm described how the positive trait of flexibility can become vicious and leave women powerless. She also discussed the idea of falling prey to the super-controlling traits needed for some long range planning.

Dottie Lamm compared the Roman god Janus to the perplexity faced by women as they attempt to make plans for living. Janus possessed a second face so that he could look in two directions at once. Lamm says that Janus probably looked backward from January (the month named after Janus) to December and forward to February seeking to make plans for a productive year. While pondering the issue of the two faces on our human attempts at planning, Lamm found that Gloria Steinem had written in a 1980 essay called "The Time Factor" that "planning ahead is a measure of class. The rich and even the middle class plan for future generations, but the poor can plan ahead only a few weeks or days." I suggest that you will need the new skill that you develop as you examine your special needs, wants, and interests and the two faces on the dilemma planning.

What is your bottom line? Do you seek planning because it is an inherited characteristic of middle class status: Do you plan because you need some new direction, bolder horizons, and more joy in your life? Dottie showed one positive side of long range planning in a Steinem quote which pointed how the women's movement itself could fail due not to lack of commitment but to lack of long range planning. Steinem said that "as a movement, women have become painfully conscious of too much reaction and living from one emergency to the next, with too little initiative and planning action of our town; hence many of our losses to a much smaller but more entrenched and consistent Right Wing."

You can reduce your emergencies and your frustrations with the use of social networking, and long and short range planning. Though pursuit of your goals might need to be done alone, you need not be lonely during that process. Remember the wisdom in the statement that the job is not everything. Some folk have advised me that "we do not have to sweat the small stuff." I find that if we sweat the small stuff by making decisions based on those truths that we have about what we really want, we may not have to stew over the big stuff. I love to hear people say that they always knew they'd be an auto mechanic, or an actor, or an engineer. They usually tell an interesting story about how they did "sweat the small stuff" and the big stuff came in manageable and powerful packages.

Blacks and Browns: Working Together

Dear Martha,

As a Black male manager, working in a utilities company, I frequently find myself making assignments to and evaluating the work of Black, Brown and Caucasian workers. The Caucasian workers do not like taking orders from me and often grumble and cause disagreements. However, I seem to spend even more time helping the Black and Brown workers patch up petty squabbles and get back on track without jeopardizing their careers. What is wrong with these minority workers? What can I do as a manager to relax some of these tensions? Are there any advantages to harmonious working relationships between Blacks and Browns that I could share with them in order to foster cooperation?

V.C. — Denver

Your questions seek understanding and illumination for a problem that has been restless, yet closeted for a long time. Despite the range of significance of the individual histories of both minority groups, they are still perceived as tokens in the workplace. You have only to observe Caucasian managers, directors and supervisors, as they wring their hands and contemplate "Where would we ever find one (a minority worker, that is) who meets the high standards of our organization?" Or, you could just recall that your presence in the workplace is the direct result of demands made by Civil Rights activists and the accomplishments of affirmative action programs.

History is clear on the fact that there are no examples of Hispanic or Black persons who became financially independent or who gained fortunes because of their opposition to other Hispanics or Blacks. Just as people do not acquire wealth while working for someone, nor do minority workers advance because another minority is held back or disenfranchised.

In Paula Gidding's book, *When and Where I Enter,* she advances the opinion that minority working against minority is ridiculous. Giddings examines statements made by Mary Church Terrell about the controversial Black educator and Dean at Howard University, Kelly Miller. Miller saw suffrage for Black women as something whose "status is not contemplated as normal social relation." Perhaps it was Miller whom Mary Church Terrell had in mind when she said, "For an intelligent colored man to oppose suffrage is the most preposterous and ridiculous thing in the world." It is just as preposterous and ridiculous for Blacks and Browns to oppose each other in the workplace.

Part of your struggle is that you experience some guilt and resentment each time this problem surfaces. You identify with the ethnic background of the parties involved. You are challenged to see your staff fail to communicate and advance. Also you feel "but by grace, there go I." Further, you probably reason that you may give expression to the same personal biases and failures. Also, any person would find it difficult to work with such a role model for conflict present in their work environment.

It would only be natural for the manager to feel some blame for the conflict or at least some responsibilty for finding resolution to the conflict. Based on our understanding of the military model of management, "Isn't controlling conflict what your job is about as a manager?"

I suggest that you seek assistance from a human relations specialist who is able to conduct simulations. Your staff could benefit from human relations training that simulates access to power, the differences between influence and position title, negotiating in the workplace, and the use of power within organizations. Your minority workers would then face the fierceness of the feelings and the subtleties of the harsh conflict as they act out being crushed by the weight of institutional racism in the neo-racist power structure. The simulations would force the staff to experience the limitations in their performance and productivity.

You might find activities for minority workers that would establish healthy competition among staff members. You might decide to use the same spirit of competition where you encourage more experimentation, encourage more trial-and-error, permit small failures and allow some duplication and overlap while you maintain an informal environment that is rich with information.

Minority workers have been handicapped by the lack of access, power and opportunity traditionally in the world of work.

Kanter in her research documents that people who have low opportunity, power and proportion in organizations are adversely affected in the workplace. She found that minority workers seemed to exhibit behaviors such as low self-esteem, limited aspirations with regard to competence, and they had a horizontal orientation that allowed them to compare themselves only with their peers. Kanter found that minority group workers foster lower group morale, try to restrict opportunities for others to grow, and show more controlling and critical behaviors.

Where Kanter examined groups and/or persons in organizations who had high opportunity, power, and proportion, their behaviors tended to be those which demonstrated high aspirations and self-esteem, an overrating of their competence, vertical orientation in which they compared themselves upward, and involvement in active change-oriented forms of protests. So, one might assume that self-hate has again raised its ugly head when Blacks and Browns attack each other instead of seeking upward mobility and change.

Another goal or objective that you may adopt as a manager is to encourage your Black and Brown staff to present themselves as if they truly support each other. There are some advantages to being viewed as persons who enjoy team membership at some point within the organization. In my book, *Tools for Survival*, Tool #13 says, "It is helpful to have a concerned minority or woman worker to provide support and direction. Minority workers must stay alert for and must discover ways of gaining broad organizational support . . . This tool really guides you to learn to fit in by seeking team membership wherever you find that you share the same interests."

You asked about the positive aspects of harmonious working relationships between Brown and Black workers. My book sets forth four stages of team membership, namely: candidate, finalist, team member, and selected team member. Team members gain commitment and approval from others, receive more attention, function with clear-cut tasks, may function as a leader, may become influence brokers, and may gain special class protections. Any of these conditions would add to the success of any worker.

Last but not least you should remind minority workers that we have too few opportunities to exercise influence. The question should be asked can we afford the dilution of our meager influence capabilities by intragroup strife. Since racism and sexism will not go away, Black and Brown workers will need each other as protectors, mentors, influence brokers, information gatherers, heroes and heroines, and champions who pull each other up as they climb.

Surviving Backlash in Corporate U.S.A.

Dear Martha,

What about this backlash in corporate America that has caused the shocking levels of reduction-in-force and retrenchment for minorities and women? Do Caucasian workers hold serious beliefs about reverse discrimination? I observe Caucasian males and females in my corporation who plod through their days with a "lackluster" performance. Yet, we [minorities and women] are being demoted, ousted and displaced in record numbers for "needing to find our skills," or "budget reductions," or "reorganization," or "new program focus," or "not appearing to fit in," or "lack of seniority," and on and on. Am I observing two separate reward and reinforcement systems at work under the same roof? You know, I once said

*with reckless abandon that "I came here looking for work, so it is no
big deal for me to find a j-o-b!" But, now . . .???*

                                        H.D. — Montbello

Dear H.D.:

Once upon a time . . . of course, we really could boast that one
could always find a job. We can still find work. But, as we look at
society's "megatrends," we know that we must use non-traditional
job search strategies. Finding work sometimes means making your
own job. I'm thinking of the high tech entrepreneurs in the
computer industry and the new airlines like People's Express and
Air Atlanta. We have just witnessed the closing of steel mills,
automaker plants, and Caterpillar. Those closings mean that some
of America's highest paid industrial workers will never work again.
Entrepreneurs who create new businesses create new jobs for
displaced workers.

John Naisbitt in his book *Megatrends* points out that our
industrial society has changed to an information society. The new
wealth, then, is no longer capital, but is rather information. The
major difference is the shift from "capital intensive" economic
development to "brain intensive" economic development, employment and training. Naisbitt cites the statistics on the entrepreneurial
explosion as an example of brain intensive economic development.
In 1980, new small businesses started at a rate of 93,000 per year. In
1982, new companies were created at the rate of about 600,000 per
year. These entrepreneurs added 6 million new workers over a seven
year period. The remaining 3 million new workers, in that same
time period, went to local and state agencies. So your future job
search would not include federal governmental agencies.

Backlash is defined as a sudden violent backward movement or a
strong adverse reaction. The word is popularly used to describe the
actions of majority persons to protect their positions from minorities.
Retrenchment means to reduce, to curtail, to cut down, and to pare
away. Davis and Watson reported the results of both phenomena in
their book *Black Life in Corporate America*. Some companies
decided that they needed a Black face at a particular spot in the
company. The token was selected and fast tracked to that specific
level. But the disadvantage was that the token was never promoted
and could not get on any traditional career path. Further, the

promotion and the token were resented by Caucasians in the corporation because here was a minority person being paid a salary higher than the majority males'. Watson and Davis report that "the guys in today's middle and top management remember how tokens were treated . . ..They are the guys who are yelling about reverse discrimination."

A Black manager who was a CPA by training, commented, "there's no such thing as reverse discrimination if you're talking about a fast track to the executive suite . . . But, I've been the affirmative action manager, the equal opportunity director, and the vice-president of special markets — not the comptroller."

Davis and Watson's interviewees saw backlash growing slowly for five or more years. "It had to come. There were too many people who were angry . . . No one wants to have to fight an equal fight for opportunities. Everyone wants an advantage and so if a White male has an advantage because of race and sex, then there's no doubt that he wants to keep that advantage. You have asked questions about a system of dualism. The duality shows minorities and women being measured by performance based criteria and job qualifications while Caucasian males are measured by the level of finesse regarding their use of the advantages that they enjoy.

In my book, *Tools for Survival*, I explore some ways to deal with the "but, now what . . .???" part of your question.

This question is a by-product of the trickle down effect of Reagonomics on women and minorities who work in corporations in America. Truly, one person's pleasure turns out to be another person's poison. It is poison that is trickling down on the jobs of minorities and women. Many of those who survive will need a good lawyer in order to maintain their positions. Tool #39 in my book states:

"Document — Do Not Lament! Practice stalking like a lion, team building like a herd, and striking like a leopard. Use concrete issues as weapons."

There are some statements that should become your action triggers. For instance, listen for "I hope you won't take this personally, but . . ." or "I hope you won't be too sensitive about this, but . . ." or the classic "I really don't want to discuss this with you, but . . ." As much as you might prefer peace and harmony, these statements alert you to prepare for warfare. Even though you'll feel embarrassed and put down, remember that at some time in the career of minority persons, most of them will need to employ an excellent attorney who has expertise in employment law. Your survival package must include funds for a legal professional you can trust to get tough on your behalf.

Paul Robeson, an extraordinary Black actor, singer, scholar, and athlete responded to the question, "but, now what . . .?" In 1920, Robeson said of his years at Rutgers University, "I wasn't just there on my own. I had to show that I could take whatever they handed out . . . This was part of our struggle." The title of Robeson's autobiography gives further testimony to the courage and faith that will be needed to survive. When asked the question, "but, now what?" Paul Robeson said, *"Here I Stand!"*

Dear Martha:

I've spent a great deal of time and money on attorney's fees and I'm so glad that I did it.

I'm writing to tell you that my career would have been ruined had I tried to finish this race alone. Please tell the brothers and sisters that this is serious business. Working in corporate America without a good labor attorney is like being in a bear fight after someone has poured honey on you.

L.A.H. — Denver

Job Evaluations and Performance Assessment

Dear Martha:

At the beginning of the year, my company conducts job evaluations and performance appraisals. This year the process is different for me because for the first time my ratings are in question. During the past four years, I received verbal approval all year long and breezed through the assessment process with extraordinary to excellent ratings. Three months ago, I started to receive some strange

feedback. You could label those exchanges warnings and complaints.
I'm ashamed to admit that the communications were so strange that
I dug in with lots of hard work, sat quietly and hoped that the weird
interactions would go away as quickly and as mysteriously as they
had come. Now, here I sit with this blank form called a job
evaluation. I'm afraid to complete the form and terrified of the
inevitable conference with my supervisor who has completed the
same form. Am I going to lose my job? What should I do to reverse
this downward spiral? What should I learn from this experience?

L.A.H. — Denver

Dear L.A.H.:

"Life is difficult . . . Once we truly know that life is difficult —
once we truly understand and accept it — then life is no longer
difficult. Because once it is accepted, the fact that life is difficult no
longer matters." This quote is found in the first paragraph of M.
Scott Peck's book entitled *The Road Less Traveled.*

Your chances for remaining with the company are definitely
threatened. Your sixth sense is giving you valid feedback. Your fear is
based on the difficulties and realities that you face. Refining,
trusting, and using your sixth sense or your strong hunches and
intuitions could have given us more time to work on your problem.
One of the things that you might learn from this experience is that
many a job has been saved by persons who turned up their ability to
correctly interpret and analyze their intuitions and hunches. I
recommend that you enroll in a seminar that teaches you skills for
building a sixth sense as a tool for survival.

Yes, you may lose your job. Now, what can you do to save
yourself? First, the most important thing to do is to take a few mental
health days. These days away from work must be used for quiet
thought and meditation. Then, you must determine the answer to
this question: "Do I want this job badly enough to fight for it?"
Everything that you do from this point forward will depend on the
answer to this question. You must get a resounding yes or no to this
question. Maybe is totally unacceptable. You'll need a solid answer
because the investment of your time, earnings, and the physical
anguish involved in this type of fight cannot be endured based on

"perhaps" or "maybe" answers.

If the answer is "no" meaning, "I don't want to remain with this company badly enough to launch a battle to stay with the fight until I win, no matter what the costs," then, you should decide how you want to leave the company. You'll want to plan for the company to pay you while you complete a job search. Also, you'll want to decide the conditions under which you would leave. For instance, you might demand and receive a decrease in pay, a transfer to another department, and three months paid vacation. Don't laugh. This is common to negotiated settlements among college administrators.

Whether your answer is "yes" or "no," you need a reputable labor attorney. Tomorrow is too late. You need the attorney *today*. Engage someone who you can trust to stay with you over the long haul. Try to find a friend who had trouble on the job, but who successfully worked with a lawyer that they would recommend. Be sure to ask your friends who are lawyers to tell you which lawyers they lose to when they handle employment disputes. Be sure to read my column from December 1984 *Odyssey West Magazine.* You cannot and should not try to launch this offensive without legal counsel. If you decide to proceed without this invaluable professional advisor, you might as well save yourself time and energy by resigning and leaving immediately. If you want this job, the cost of legal counsel must not become an issue. Beg, borrow, deal, or steal, but, get the money to pay your attorney. Consider the expenditure a long-term investment in your primary residence, pension, and health plan.

By the time you receive this response, you'll need to take care of the immediate problem; this is the conference with your supervisor. Complete the form rating yourself as high as you would have under more ordinary circumstances. Then, schedule the conference, submit *some,* not all, of the documentation of your past performance. Curb any temptation to exchange accusations. Remember, a decision has already been made to dismiss you. Keep it short, listen, take notes and *do not sign anything.*

Expect pressure tactics to make you sign the appraisal form because "the company rules require that you acknowledge the conduct of the conference." You know that from this point forward the rules will only be used when they facilitate your dismissal. You could respond that you will "consider signing after I've had time to review the results of this conference." Run, don't walk to your attorney and prepare a written response. You may, then, sign the form when you are certain that your signature only means that the conference did in fact take place and you are aware of the ratings. Your written response could include documentation that you held back during the first meeting. Also, prepare a rebuttal that includes a chronology of events and people that could refute the alleged charges and accusations. You know that those people will not want any part of this dispute, but their involvement should be noted.

Remember, you will win when you have sufficiently documented disparate treatment, and/or violation of published rules or established practices. So, keep sharp eye for and listen carefully to underground information. For example, you may learn that one of the charges made about your work is an action that has been established acceptable practice for one of your co-workers. You might have been reprimanded for using funds to pay for the airfare of a job applicant whom you want to interview. Upon investigation, you may find that three airline tickets were approved so that persons in another department could visit and interview a candidate. In addition to the airfare, three professionals received salaries for release time to conduct the interview. Such a scenario makes your expenditure much less shocking.

The downward spiral will reverse itself when your supervisor is convinced that the heat will not disappear, that the pressure will continue to build, and that the fighting will not diminish until you are victorious. Expect this realization to take at least six months. The positive side of the time expenditure is that you'll have plenty of time to develop, modify and to adjust your game plan.

I suggest that you resist the temptation to use the press because you lose control of your game plan. The press gives no guarantees for not revealing their sources or for timing the release of information. You must rely on legal redress and administrative remedies.

Another point to remember is that performance evaluations are very useful for making changes in personnel. Traditionally, the evaluation process has been heavily relied upon in order to validate changes such as non-selection, termination, or transfer.

You'll probably learn from this experience how poorly workers are prepared for the struggle to maintain employment after they get the job. You'll also learn to direct more energies toward activities outside of getting the job done. More of your energies should be directed toward establishing many mentorship relationships and positioning yourself for the fight required to stay with the company of your choice.

Khadijah Farabi-Nance provides a formula for survival in her poem:

I have become

           a celebration
of perfection
I have balanced

           out
re-examined

           the alternatives
and realized

           I am perfect
ain't even no arrogance

           involved
just a statement

           of facts
was no error

           of judgment made
on my day of birth

           you understand
I'm a perfect member of my family

           (fit right in)
perfect member of my community
perfect eyes (2)
perfect teeth
perfect skin
perfect time and space
perfect

           to be here
right now

           in this place

© Khadijah Farabi-Nance, 1984

Index

End Notes

1. Joseph Murphy, *The Power of Your Subconscious Mind* (New Jersey: Prentice-Hall, 1963), p. 47.
2. Norman Vincent Peale, *The Power of Positive Thinking* (New York: Foundation for Christian Living, 1978), p. 1.
3. Florence Scovel Shinn, *The Game of Life and How to Play It* (New York: Gerald Rickard, 1941, p. 14.
4. Ibid., p. 14.
5. Ernest Holmes, *The Science of Mind Textbook* (Los Angeles: United Church of Religious Science, 1946), p. 164.
6. Norman Vincent Peale, *The Power of Positive Thinking*, p. 105.
7. Chancellor Williams, *The Destruction of Black Civilization*, Chicago, Third World Press, 1976.
8. E. Parke Gibson, *The $70 Billion in the Black: America's Black Consumer* (New York: Macmillan Book Co.), 1978.
9. E. Franklin Frazier, *Black Bourgeoisie*.
10. Milton Kramer, *Sleep Disorders* (Ohio: University of Cincinnati College of Medicine), 1979.
11. William H. Grier and Price M. Cobbs, *Black Rage* (New York: Basic Books, 1968), p. 102.
12. Meg Wheatley, "How to Get Your Job Promoted," *Ms. Magazine*, July, 1981, pp. 85-87.
13. Ibid., p. 87.
14. Earl Conrad, *The Invention of the Negro* (New York: Paul S. Eriksson), 1966, pp. 86-87.
15. U.S. Bureau of the Census, Money Income in 1977 of Families and Persons in U.S. Series P-60, No. 118 (Washington, D.C.: U.S. Government Printing Office), 1979.
16. William Raspberry, "Job Expectations Are Unrealistic," *The Washington Post Co.*, 1981.
17. Michael Korda, "When Business Becomes Bloodsport," *Playboy*, 1981, p. 262.
18. Patricia O'Brien, "Women Opting for Blue Collar Jobs," *The Denver Post*, January 9, 1982.
19. Mary Lindenstein Walshok, *Blue Collar Women: Pioneers on the Male Frontier* (New York: Feminists Press), 1982.
20. Op. cit., Kanter, pp. 240-249.
21. Op. cit., Korda, p. 264.
22. Herbert A. Simon, *Administrative Behavior* (New York: The Free Press, 1976), pp. 6-9.
23. Robert Presthus, *Organizational Society* (New York: St. Marten's Press, 1978), p. 1.
24. Betty Lehan Harragan, *Games Mother Never Taught You: Corporate Gamesmanship for Women* (New York: Warner Books, 1977), p. 24.
25. Rosabeth Moss Kanter, *Men and Women of the Corporation* (New York: Basic Books, Inc., 1977), pp. 248-249.
26. Op. cit., Kanter, p. 210.
27. Op. cit., Kanter, p. 212.
28. Susan Fraker, "Why Women Aren't Getting to the Top," Fortune April 16, 1984, pp. 40-45.
29. Ibid., Fraker: pp. 40-45.
30. Op. cit., Kanter, p. 210.
31. Op. cit., Kanter, p. 210.
32. Adele Scheele, "Beyond Ability: Developing Success Competencies for Making It," *Educational Horizons*, Volume 58, Number 3, Spring, 1980, p. 134.
33. Ibid., p. 135.
34. Ibid., p. 135.
35. Ibid., p. 136.
36. Ibid., p. 136.
37. Ibid., p. 137.

38. Ibid., p. 136.

39. Ibid., p. 136.

40. Ibid., p. 136.

41. Ibid., p. 138.

42. Op. cit., Harragan, p. 29.

43. Carol Kleiman, "Does Sisterhood Stop at the Top," *MS.*, March, 1981, p. 92.

44. Gloria Steinem, "How to Survive Burnout, Reagan, and Daily Life," *MS.*, February, 1982. p. 96.

45. Marilyn Moats Kennedy, "Office Politics and Career Knockouts," (Illinois, Multimedia Product Development, 1980).

46. Marilyn Machlowitz, "The Great Imposter," *Working Woman*, February, 1982, pp. 97-98.

47. Kate Vozoff, "Getting Along and Getting Ahead," *Equal Opportunity Forum*, Vol. 9, Number 4, February, 1982, p. 16.

48. Op. cit., Steinem, p. 96.

49. *Rocky Mountain News*, Wednesday, March 3, 1982, p. 42.

50. Isaiah J. Poole, "If Acronyms Could Cure," *Black Enterprise*, June, 1980, p. 101.

51. Orrin E. Klapp, *Collective Search for Identity* (New York: 1969), pp. 5-6.

52. Richard H. Stansfield, *The Best Ever How-To-Get-A-Job Book* (Pennsylvania: Chilton Book Company, 1980), p. 77.

53. Ibid., Stansfield, p. 92.

54. Sylvia Porter, "Looking for a Job? Sharpen Up Interview Technique," *Denver Post*, Sunday, January, 1982.

55. Ibid., Porter.

56. Barbara Swaby, "The Role of the Black Woman in Colorado." Speech given at the 2nd Conference of Education and Employment of Black Women, June, 1981.

57. Ibid., Swaby, Speech.

58. Marilyn Moats Kennedy, "Status and Perks and a Fistful of Dollars," *Savvy*, December, 1981, pp. 37-38.

59. Sherry Chastain, "On the Job: The Winning Interview," *Working Woman*, October, 1981, pp. 30-34.

60. John Illick and Barbara Schindler Jones, *Successful Negotiating Skills for Women* (New York: Playboy Publications, 1981), pp. 41-58.

61. Doug Shepard, "Questions to Ask an Interviewer," *Black Collegian*, March, 1982, pp. 80-82.

62. John P. Fernandez, *Black Managers in White Corporations* (New York: John Wiley and Sons).

63. Ibid., Fernandez, p. 193.

64. Ibid., Fernandez, p. 194.

65. Ibid., Fernandez, p. 195.

66. Ibid., Fernandez, p. 196.

67. Ibid., Fernandez, p. 197.

68. Ibid., Fernandez, p. 217.

69. *Newsday: The Long Island Newspaper*, December 19, 1968, p. 47.

70. William H. Grier and Price M. Cobbs, *Black Rage* (New York: Basic Books Inc.), 1968, pp. 103-104.

71. Amal Nag, "Women and Minorities Lose Ground in Slump," *Wall Street Journal*, June 21, 1981, p. 3.

72. Op. cit., Grier and Cobbs, p. 105.

73. Catherine Ettlinger, "Taking Charge On Your Job," *Savvy*, April, 1980. p. 16.

74. Ibid., Ettlinger, pp. 16-18.

75. Op. cit., Vozoff, p. 16.

76. Ibid., Vozoff, p. 17.

77. Johathan Kaufman, "Rights Frontier," *Wall Street Journal*, Wednesday, July 9, 1980, p. 1.

78. Staff of Catalyst, "The Luck Factor at Work," *Working Woman*, October, 1982, pp. 75-78.

79. Kenneth Roman and Joel Raphaelson, "Writing It Up," *Working Woman*, August, 1981, p. 82.

80. Tobie Sullivan, "On the Job: The Memo," *Working Woman*, August, 1981, p. 16.

81. Ibid., Sullivan, p. 16.

82. Marty Meitus, "Togetherness," *Rocky Mountain News*, Monday, August 10, 1981.

83. Ibid., Meitus, p. 16.

84. Ibid., Meitus, p. 16.

85. Jennifer S. Macleod, "Outwit the Squeeze-Out," *Savvy*, February, 1982, p. 77.

86. Ibid., Macleod, pp. 78-80.

87. Karen Noelle Clark and Diane McCarty, "Getting Fired: A Turning Point, Not a Dead End," *Essence*, September, 1981, p. 28.

88. Betty Lehan Harragan, *Knowing the Score* (New York: St. Martin's Press, 1983), p. 6.

89. John Fernandez, *Racism and Sexism in Corporate Life.* (Massachusetts: Lexington Books, 1981), p. 8.

90. Ibid., Fernandez, p. 8.

91. Hans Selye, *Stress Without Distress*, (New York: New American Library, 1974).

92. Ibid., Selye.

93. Walter McQuade and Ann Aikman, *Stress: What It Is, What It Can Do To Your Health, How To Fight Back* (New York: E. P. Dutton, 1974).

94. Jerry Greenwald, *Be The Person You Were Meant To Be: Your Best Friend Is You* (New York: Dell Publishing Co., 1973).

95. Donald A. Tubesing, *Stress Skills* (Oakbrook, Illinois, Whole Person Associates, 1979).

96. Op. cit., McQuade and Aikman.

97. Op. cit., Tubesing.

98. T. H. Holmes and R. H. Rahe, "Social Readjustment Rating Scale," *Journal of Psychosomatic Research*, Vol. 11, 1967, p. 216.

99. Jessie Muse, *Survival of Stressed Teachers*, NEA, 1980.

100. Sheila Ostrander and Lynn Schroeder, *Superlearning* (New York: Delacorte Press, 1979).

101. M. Scott Peck, M.D., *The Road Less Traveled*, (New York: Simon & Schuster Inc., 1978).